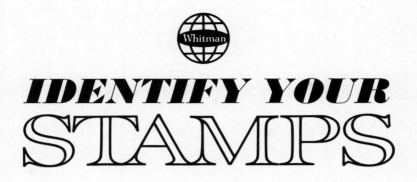

IDENTIFY YOUR STAMPS

by

ERVIN J. FELIX

COVER DESIGN
MEL HAAG

WHITMAN PUBLISHING COMPANY
(a subsidiary of Western Publishing Company, Inc.)
RACINE, WISCONSIN

6723

TABLE OF CONTENTS

Introduction

STAMPS ARE THE WINDOWS
OF THE HISTORY OF THE WORLD!

In order to appreciate how vast an era of civilization is portrayed in the designs used in the wide world of postage stamps, it is really necessary to have reasonably complete and thoroughly illustrated information readily available.

It was the intention of the author to present this work in an easily read and understood format by including as many illustrations, drawings, sketches and maps as would benefit both the new collector and the advanced collector.

While every phase of stamp identification could not possibly be properly covered in one book, it is hoped that those items selected for illustrating and those subjects chosen to be discussed will meet with the general approval of all collectors and dealers.

HAPPY HUNTING!

CREDITS

The author wishes to express sincere thanks to the following people for their help and enthusiasm during the compilation of this book.

EARL APFELBAUM	ROBSON LOWE, LONDON
LESTER BROOKMAN	EDWARD W. METZGER, JR.
RICHARD McP. CABEEN	A. L. MICHAEL, LONDON
HAROLD COHN	PETER RICKENBACH, LONDON
SYLVESTER COLBY	S. SEREBRAKIAN
ALEXANDER D. GAGE	NEIL SHAFER
IRVING LAPINER	ROBIN TAYLOR, LONDON
LYONS LIVINGSTON	THEO. VAN DAM

SISTER MARIANNA GEMMET

DE LA RUE DIES (Victorian and Georgian)

Types of the General Plates used by Messrs. De La Rue & Co. for printing British Colonial Stamps.

I. VICTORIAN KEY TYPE

Die I	Die II

Die I

1. The ball of decoration on the second point of the Crown appears as a dark mass of lines.
2. Dark vertical shading separates the front hair from the bun.
3. The vertical line of colour outlining the front of the throat stops at the sixth line of shading on the neck.
4. The white space in the coil of the hair above the curl is roughly the shape of a pin's head.

Die II

1. There are very few lines of colour in the ball and it appears almost white.
2. A white vertical strand of hair appears in place of the dark shading.
3. The line stops at the eighth line of shading.
4. The white space is oblong, with a line of colour partially dividing it at the left end.

II. GEORGIAN KEY TYPE

Die I

A. The second (thick) line below the name of the country is cut slanting, conforming roughly to the shape of the Crown on each side.
B. The labels of solid colour bearing the words "POSTAGE" and "& REVENUE" are square at the inner top corners.
C. There is a projecting "bud" on the outer spiral of the ornament in each of the lower corners.

Die II

A. The second line is cut vertically on each side of the Crown.
B. The labels curve inwards at the top.
C. There is no "bud" in this position.

— 5 —

READING AND USING A STAMP CATALOGUE

While most all stamp catalogues follow reasonably the same style and format, a few words about what all the numbers and dates mean will probably add to the interest of a newcomer to this great hobby.

The following illustration is a portion of a page from the new American edition of the Gibbons-Whitman Postage Stamp Catalogue, Part I, United States and Possessions, United Nations and British Commonwealth.

In the illustration, "A" refers to where the catalogue number of the stamp is found, which is the basis for all checklists, references, etc. "B" refers to the illustration number of the stamp; stamps are illustrated in the catalogue in order to guide the collector to the proper identification of the stamp. "C" refers to the face value of the stamp, "D" refers to the description of the color or colors in which the stamp was printed, and, in certain cases, an italicized type on the same line will indicate the color of the paper upon which the stamp design was printed. "E" refers to the catalogue valuation of the stamp in mint or unused condition. "F" refers to the valuation of the stamp in used or cancelled condition.

1959 (19 June). *Recess; values typo. in black.*
P 11 × 10½.

D 87	D 5	½ c. scarlet ..	..	5	5
D 88	,,	1 c. scarlet ..	..	5	5
		va. " 1 " omitted	..	$150	
		vb. " 1 CENT "			
		omitted ..	..	$150	
D 89	,,	2 c. scarlet ..	..	6	6
D 90	,,	3 c. scarlet ..	..	7	5
D 91	,,	4 c. scarlet ..	..	10	5
D 92	,,	5 s. scarlet ..	..	12	7
D 93	,,	6 c. scarlet ..	..	12	7
D 94	,,	7 c. scarlet ..	..	14	7
D 95	,,	8 c. scarlet ..	..	17	7
D 96	,,	10 c. scarlet ..	..	18	7
D 97	,,	30 c. scarlet ..	..	60	9
D 98	,,	50 c. scarlet ..	..	95	9
D 99	,,	$1 scarlet ..	..	1.80	11
D100	,,	$5 scarlet ..	..	7.50	20

D5

1959 (19 June). *Recess; values typo. in black.* P11 x 10½.

A	B	C D		E	F
D 87	D5	½ c. scarlet ..	..	5	5
D 88	"	1 c. scarlet ..	..	5	5
		va. "1" omitted	..	$150	
		vb. "1 CENT"			
		omitted ..	..	$150	
D 89	"	2 c. scarlet ..	..	6	6
D 90	"	3 c. scarlet ..	..	7	5
D 91	"	4 c. scarlet ..	..	10	5
D 92	"	5 s. scarlet ..	..	12	7
D 93	"	6 c. scarlet ..	..	12	7
D 94	"	7 c. scarlet ..	..	14	7
D 95	"	8 c. scarlet ..	..	17	7
D 96	"	10 c. scarlet ..	..	18	7
D 97	"	30 c. scarlet ..	..	60	9
D 98	"	50 c. scarlet ..	..	95	9
D 99	"	$1 scarlet ..	..	1.80	11
D100	"	$5 scarlet ..	..	7.50	20

1¢ 1851 TYPE I

Below the "ONE CENT" label there is a curved line, and the scrolls are complete.

1¢ 1851 TYPE IA

Similar to type I except top ornaments and curved line are cut.

1¢ 1851 TYPE IB

Similar to type I except balls and scrolls below lower label are cut off.

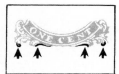

1¢ 1851 TYPE II

Side ornaments complete. Balls and ornaments at bottom cut off.

1¢ 1851 TYPE III

Curved line at top and bottom center are cut off. Ornaments on sides complete.

1¢ 1851 TYPE IIIA

Same as III except either top or bottom outer line is broken in center.

1¢ 1851 TYPE IV

Same as II except top or bottom curved lines are recut.

1¢ 1857

Perf. 15, same design as the 1851 issue. Portions of side ornaments are cut away.

3¢ 1851 TYPE I

Outside frame line on top and on bottom.

3¢ 1851 TYPE II

Outer frame line at top and bottom off. Side lines of frame recut from top to bottom.

3¢ 1851 TYPE IIA

Frame lines at side run only from top to bottom of design.

5¢ 1856 TYPE I

Projections show on all four sides.

5¢ 1856 TYPE II

Projections are cut away somewhat on top and bottom.

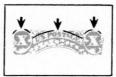

10¢ 1855 TYPE I

Top outer line and "X" (both) are broken. Shells and outer line below almost complete.

10¢ 1855 TYPE II

Design on top not broken. Side ornaments not broken. 3 pearls at bottom, each side.

10¢ 1855 TYPE III

Outer line and "Xs" cut on top. Bottom outer line and shells partly cut.

10¢ 1855 TYPE IV

Outer lines at top and bottom have been re-cut.

10¢ 1855 TYPE V

Side ornaments cut some. Outer lines are complete except over top right "X." One pearl on most.

15¢ 1869 TYPE I

Picture design has no frame line.

15¢ 1869 TYPE II

Picture design has a frame line.

1¢ 1873

A small dash appears in pearl left of numeral "1."

2¢ 1873

A small diagonal dash is under scroll left of "U.S."

1¢ 1881-82 TYPE B

Upper part of stamp is recut. Upper arabesques has added shading.

3¢ 1873
Heavy shading under upper tail of left ribbon.

3¢ 1881
Shading on sides of oval cut ½ of original width.

6¢ 1873
There are four heavy shading lines at lower part of left ribbon.

6¢ 1882
On either side of the portrait are 3 vertical lines instead of the original 4.

7¢ 1873
Lower right ball has 2 semicircles at outline ends.

10¢ 1873
Scroll at right side of upper label has a small semicircle.

10¢ 1882
There are 4 vertical lines between portrait oval and shield edge.

12¢ 1873
In the figure "2" the scroll balls are crescent shaped.

15¢ 1873
Shows a "V" made by recutting 2 lines in upper left triangle.

2¢ 1894 TYPE I
Horizontal lines are of same thickness throughout design.

2¢ 1894 TYPE II
Horizontal lines are thinner inside of inner triangle.

2¢ 1894 TYPE III
Same as type II except lines do not cross inside of triangles.

$1 1895 TYPE I
Circles are broken by white curved line under "ONE DOLLAR."

$1 1895 TYPE II
The $1 circles are completed (no breaks).

10¢ 1898 TYPE I
Tip of the ornaments around "10" does not break into white circle around "TEN CENTS."

10¢ 1898 TYPE II
Tips of the ornaments break into the white border around "TEN CENTS."

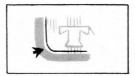

2¢ 1903 DIE I
Thin, curved line around "T," lower left.

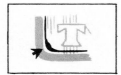

2¢ 1903 DIE II
Curved line around lower left "T" is heavier, with gouge.

2¢ 1912 TYPE I
Each ribbon has shading line. Toga button is faint. Top of toga rope is faint. Face shading lines.

2¢ 1912 TYPE IA
Stronger lines than type I. Toga button, rope and shading is heavier.

2¢ 1912 TYPE II
Lines of the toga are heavy. Shading on face forms strong curved line.

2¢ 1912 TYPE III
The curved ribbons each have 2 lines.

2¢ 1912 TYPE IV
Top of toga rope cut. Toga button forms "ᑕID." Left 2 is thin.

2¢ 1912 TYPE V

Toga line is complete.
5 shading lines in toga
button. Left "2" is
broken. Shading dots
on nose.

2¢ 1912 TYPE VA

3rd row of dots from
bottom has 4 instead
of 6 on nose. Height is
shorter than type V.

2¢ 1912 TYPE VI

Same as type V except
line in left "2" is
heavy.

2¢ 1912 TYPE VII

Heavy left "2." Dots
added to top of head.
An extra row of dots
was added to the upper
lip.

3¢ 1908 TYPE I

Toga rope and shading
is weak. 5th line from
left missing. Thin line
on lips.

3¢ 1908 TYPE II

Toga rope and shading
is heavy. Heavy lip
line.

3¢ 1908 TYPE III

5th shading line is
missing. Middle line in
toga button has two
dashes with dot. "PO"
is separated by line.
Frame line is complete.

3¢ 1908 TYPE IV

Shading is complete on
toga. Lines are broken
in toga button. "PO"
letters are joined.
Frame line is broken.

2¢ 1923 TYPE I

Hair lines at top of
head are thin. No line
on left of forehead.
Left scroll faint top
and left.

2¢ 1929 TYPE II

Heavy hair lines on top
of head. Heavy line to
left of forehead. Scroll
at left has heavy out-
line on left.

THE FRAMELINES OF THE BICOLORED STAMPS OF DENMARK AND DANISH WEST INDIES

A master die was prepared for these first bicolored stamps of Denmark and the Danish West Indies. The following drawings show the types of frames and frame lines, varieties of which are much sought after by specialists.

Thick frame line found on all of 48 skilling values.

Thin frame line found on skilling values except the 48 sk. Also found on the cent and ore values.

Thick vertical curved part of arabesque design also found on 48 skilling values.

Thin vertical curved part of arabesque design found on skilling values except the 48 sk. Also found on the cent and ore values.

Oval clear of arabesque.

These enlarged frame and oval lines show an easy-to-find position of the normal and the inverted frames.

Oval touches arabesque.

Enlarged drawing of detail of the normal arabesque.

Enlarged drawing of detail of the arabesque with inverted frame.

PHILATELIC ODDITIES

Double Overprint,
One Inverted

Double Surcharge

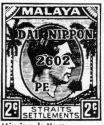

Missing Letters

Inverted Center

Security Paper

Varnish Bars

Burelage

German Printed
Propaganda, WWII
Note Star over King
Hammer-Sickle upper left

IMPERIAL RUSSIAN STAMPS
AND THE REVOLUTION
1917-1922

In 1913 the Imperial Russian government honored the 300th anniversary of the royal family of Romanov with a set of commemorative stamps. Four short years later in 1917, the Czar of all the Russias, Nicholas II Romanov, was forced to abdicate and the following year he and his entire family were murdered in Ekaterinburg.

The Kremlin, Moscow

Czar Nicholas II

Romanov Castle, Moscow

The revolution brought about complete chaos throughout all of the vast territory of Russia; some of the czarist Russian army and navy officers tried to preserve the dignity of imperial rule and they led sometimes rather pitiful and ragged armies of men and refugees in what proved to be a futile attempt at a semblance of independence.

Stamps of the former Imperial Russian government which portrayed the coat of arms of the royal house of Romanov and some of the Romanov Commemorative issues were surcharged and overprinted for use in the newly independent districts and areas, as well as by the various military commanders who resisted the march of the revolutionists.

Provisional Government

Northwestern Army, General Yudenich

Imperial Russian Stamps, Continued

Northern Army
General Rodzianko

Siberian Government of
Admiral Kolchak

Far Eastern Republic
General Semenov

Western Army (Latvia)
Colonel Bermondt-Avalov

Internees Government
General Wrangel

South Russia
General Denikin

South Russia
Crimea Regional Government

South Russia
Don Cossack Government

South Russia
Kuban Cossack Government

Siberia
Priamur Province

Imperial Russian Stamps, Continued

Armenia National Republic

Transcaucasian Federated Republics

Ukraine National Republic

These stamps and their cancellations make a fascinating study as a stamp collection as well as a vibrant parade of the history of the era, as can be noted from the above illustrations of basic issues without going into any of the varieties, errors, etc.

Cancel:
Chalangtung in
Manchuria

Cancel:
Urga in
Mongolia

TRIDENT OVERPRINTS

With the collapse of the Imperial Russian Empire in 1917 many areas within Russia set up independent governments. While most of them had stamps overprinted for local use only, the Trident overprints of the Ukraine were more generally used. There are many types, varieties and colors of these Ukranian overprints, and the following drawings indicate basic types used:

Vienna issue on stamps of Austria

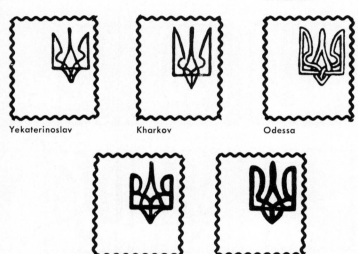

Yekaterinoslav   Kharkov   Odessa

Odessa

Types of Trident overprints used in the Ukraine on stamps of Russia, these being the first issues of the Ukranian Republic, 1918. Many varieties exist.

Ukraine

Trident Overprints, Continued

Odessa, Machine Printed

Odessa, Hand Stamped

Kharkov, Kopecks
and Rubles

Poltava

Yekaterinovslav

Poltava

On Kopecks

On Rubles

POSTAL SYSTEMS DURING WARTIME

During the years from 1840 to the present time there have been many wars, invasions, occupations and skirmishes which have changed the course of history. Many of these momentous events have left their indelible mark in philately through the overprinted and surcharged stamps used by the occupation forces, as well as specially designed and printed stamps for the use of the population in the occupied areas.

Practically all nations are geared to handle emergency mail during periods of stress and crises, but when complete chaos strikes, as occurs when one country overruns and militarily occupies another, which happened in the Franco-Prussian War of 1870-1871, the Boer War of 1898-1900, World War I from 1914-1918, World War II from 1939-1945, etc., then we have a more vivid postal picture.

A few graphic examples of what developed in the stamp and cancellation category during various types of military occupation periods are illustrated here. There are many more illustrations to be found in the alphabetical arrangement of the stamp illustrations section of this book.

Siege of Mafeking

Austrian Occ.
Montenegro

Italian Occ.
Austria

Postal Systems During Wartime, Continued

German Occ.
Luxembourg

Belgian Occ.
Germany

Finnish Occ.
Russia

Confederate States

Spanish Civil War

Japanese Occ.
Burma

Thai Occ. Malaya

Greek Occ. Turkey

WAR TAX STAMPS

Because of the far greater expense of operating various governmental agencies during war time as well as the cost of the military, many countries resorted to a special war tax on all postal matter to obtain additional revenue. This most interesting topic of stamp collecting is known in the form of a specially surcharged and/or overprinted stamp as well as specially designed stamps for the purpose of collecting the additional war tax. The following illustrations depict some of the various stamp designs, surcharges and overprints so used.

British Empire World War I

War Tax Stamps, Continued

Macao & Timor
Portuguese Colonies, 1919

Mozambique
Port Colony 1916-18

North Borneo
Br. Colony WWII

Portugal 1919

Port. Guinea 1919

Port. India 1919

Puerto Rico
Spanish Colony 1898

Spain
1874

1876

1879

Spain
1897

1898

Timor 1919

POSTAGE STAMPS NEGOTIABLE AS COINS

Shortages of metal, business men's ingenuity and the need to keep the economic road open, led to the issuing of encased and mounted postage stamps to fill the need for small denominational coins. The following illustrations depict a few types of this emergency material:

UNITED STATES	AUSTRIA
DENMARK	FRANCE
GERMANY	ITALY
NORWAY	SPAIN

CERTIFICATE OF GUARANTEE

A certificate which guarantees the genuineness of a specific stamp or surcharge or overprint on a stamp is a most important requisite when a collector or investor is about to buy a rare or high catalogue stamp. It has been known to happen to the unwary that they bought a counterfeit stamp and that the counterfeit was so expertly done that not even the collector or the dealer could detect the difference from the genuine item. Most dealers would want a certificate with the stamp if they were buying it over the counter or would want one if it was sold to them through auction.

There are various committees of true experts and specialists who are able to detect these counterfeits because they have studied the background of stamp production and they specialize in the many phases of philately which would make the counterfeit stand out to them. There are many instances on record where the specialists have even been able to identify the counterfeit stamp to the name of the man who did the work such as Sperati, Fournier, etc. The illustration on the opposite page is that of a certificate from the Philatelic Foundation in New York of this stamp.

In 1937 the Venezuelan postal authorities had a very small quantity of the 40¢ indigo stamp of 1932 depicting Simon Bolivar overprinted and surcharged as a 25¢ denomination. This is an illustration of the rare double surcharge.

No. 15,558   May 7th 19 62

THE PHILATELIC FOUNDATION
22 EAST 35TH STREET
NEW YORK 16, N.Y.

EXPERT COMMITTEE

We have examined the enclosed   Venezuela

1937 25c/40c indigo Scott #319 used with

double overprint -

submitted by

of which a photograph is attached and are of the opinion

that the double overprint is genuine - - - - - - - -

For The Expert Committee
Chairman

THEY LOOK ALIKE . . . BUT!

Look closely at the illustrations shown on these two pages and note the striking similarity yet the obvious differences where indicated. Both Finland and Poland were under Imperial Russian influence for centuries before postage stamps made their appearance; Finland as a Grand Duchy and Poland as a kingdom within the Russian Empire.

Imperial
Russia

Gd. Duchy
Finland

Dominion
Poland

Russia

Finland

Russia

Finland

Russia

Finland

Russia

Finland

Russia

Finland

Russia

Finland

They Look Alike . . . But!, Continued

Russia

Finland

Russia

Finland

Russia

Finland

Russia

Finland

Russia

Finland

PHILATELICALLY ILLUSTRATED. . . .
DID YOU KNOW . . . ?

In all the wide world of postage stamps there remain hidden away just hundreds of discoveries! Illustrated herewith are some seldom noted designs which were found at random while browsing through a nice general worldwide stamp collection. These are only a very few different designs; practically every collector can show additional and equally interesting different designs.

Turkey—
Trojan Horse

Uganda—
X-Ray Machine

Cuba—
Fingerprint

St. Thomas & Pr.—
Scuba Diving

Switzerland—
Petrified Fish

Norway—
First Norwegian Plane

Pitcairn Islands—
H.M.S. Bounty Bible

Northern Rhodesia—
Modern Error
Value Omitted

United Arab Republic—
Braille Reading

Czechoslovakia—
American Indian

Ajman—
Stanley-Gibbons Stamp
Centenary

Austria—
World's Largest
Ferris Wheel

Paper Money on
Stamps

Monaco—
Glass Coffin of
Bernadette of Lourdes

Austria—
Page from First Edition
of the Lutheran Bible

ISSUES OF IMPERIAL CHINESE GOVERNMENT POST, 1897

In 1896 the Imperial Chinese Government ordered the Customs Post changed to the National Post and that dollar values be used effective January 1, 1897. The shortage of postage stamps which developed prior to the new stamps being available caused the government to print and surcharge stamps of various issues and denominations to conform to the imperial edict, as illustrated (enlarged).

Bronze Container,
1750-1111 B.C.

Foochow Issue, 1912. Issued to indicate the neutrality of the post office during the Chinese Revolution.

Nanking Issue, 1912. Issued to indicate the neutrality of the post office of the Republic of China.

CHALON PORTRAIT OF QUEEN VICTORIA
Original Painting

This painting was given to Albert, Prince Consort, by the Queen herself. The Prince Consort had a copy made for the great exhibition at the famous Crystal Palace in 1851, to insure against any loss or damage to the original. However, this wonderful painting has since disappeared. It was last seen at a London Exhibition in 1897, and to this day it has never been located.

CHALON PORTRAIT OF QUEEN VICTORIA
Buckley Copy

PHOTO COURTESY OF ROBSON LOWE OF LONDON, ENGLAND

The artist John Buckley was commissioned to do a copy of the famous Chalon Portrait so that it would be ready before the great exhibition in the Crystal Palace in London in 1851. There was not the attention to detail or delicate features in the Buckley copy as there was in the Chalon original. The Prince Consort sold the Buckley copy after the close of the exhibition. This painting had more than one owner, and today it is in Windsor Castle.

CHALON PORTRAIT OF QUEEN VICTORIA

It was Alfred Edward Chalon, R.A. (Painter in Water Colours) of Geneva, Switzerland, who, in 1837 painted that most gracious full length portrait of the young, attractive, brilliant and delightful Queen Victoria.

It was Samuel Cousins who made the finest engraving from this portrait, replicas of which are found throughout the British Empire to this day. The Cousins engraving was of such character as to be that engraving from which the finest of the now famous Chalon portrait postage stamp designs were made starting in 1851 with the Canadian classic, the 12 pence black. Following this, Canada also issued the 7½ pence green in 1857 and the 12½¢ green in 1859:

The following are other adaptations of this famous portrait by different British Colonies:

Queen Victoria was born Georgianna Charlotte Augusta Alexandrina Victoria, May 24, 1819, the daughter of Edward, Duke of Kent, and Victoria, Princess of Saxe-Coburg. She became Queen June 20, 1837, ruled for more than 63 years and died January 22, 1901.

PIGEON POST

Aerial messengers in the form of pigeons are known to history as far back as about 1500 BC when they were used by the ancient Greeks as a means to announce the winners of the Olympic Games. Even the great financiers of the 19th century took advantage of the speed of the homing pigeon to gain advance information over their competitors. From Baghdad to Syria and Egypt there was established a line of communication in the 12th century. Pigeon communication was also established between the islands of Java and Sumatra in the Dutch East Indies during the early part of the 19th century.

During the Franco-Prussian War of 1870-1871 when Paris was besieged by the Prussian troops, pigeons were taken out of the city in the famous balloon post flights so that they could bring messages back into the city. While the balloon post was able to take messages out of the city to the Provinces, there was no way to get word back into the city except by pigeon service.

A pigeon was awarded a high military honor for services rendered during the great battle of the Argonne Forest in France, during World War I.

The first real stamps, even though of a local nature, for pigeon mail service were issued in 1898 for service between Auckland, New Zealand and the Great Barrier Island located some 65 miles northeast of Auckland. There was only a weekly ship between the Great Barrier Island and New Zealand and because of the great natural wealth of copper and mineral deposits on Great Barrier, there was definite need for faster communication between the island and New Zealand. After a trial flight staged by a pigeon fancier, the first pigeon message service was established and the first flight was on May 14, 1897. Shortly after the initial successes of this communication service, a rival company was formed on a smaller island whence emanated the second series of pigeon post stamps, this time in triangular format, 6d blue and 1/ red. The rate was 6d from the island to New Zealand, and 1/ from New Zealand to the Island of Marotiri. This entire service, known as the "Great Barrier Pigeongram Agency," ended Sept. 26, 1908, upon the successful completion of the telegraph service between Auckland, New Zealand, and the Great Barrier enterprises.

BALLOON POST OF THE SIEGE OF PARIS
DURING FRANCO-PRUSSIAN WAR 1870-71

It remained for the Franco-Prussian War of 1870-1871 to really distinguish the Balloon Post as such, even though communications via balloon methods were not unheard of prior to this time. Actually, a balloon was flown over London piloted by a certain Blanchard in 1784; in 1785 the same Blanchard flew the English Channel with mail, and in 1836 the balloon "NASSAU" flew from London to Germany. The world's first postage stamp, the Penny Black of Great Britain, was used on mail dropped over London in 1841 when the pioneer balloonist, Gelion, made this most spectacular flight.

When the Prussian Army invaded France in 1870, they aimed straight for Paris and laid siege to that great city on the 18th of September, 1870. Being well aware of the rapid advance of the Prussians, the French determined to hold their city and sent the last mail train out at 3 P.M. on September 18, and shortly thereafter the city was tightly surrounded, and the siege kept up until January 28, 1871. The ring of steel and soldiers around the city precluded any information or letters etc., from getting in or out. The besieged Parisians tried just about everything to communicate with the outside world, even to the extent of using dogs to carry messages, metal balls in the Seine river, hiding messages on volunteers who tried to get through the lines. Whatever success that was attained, can be attributed to the use of balloons which carried mail and passengers, and to carrier pigeons.

The carrier pigeon service was usually reserved for official communications; the pigeons were taken out by balloon and then when they returned to Paris, they brought information from other official sources.

The balloon post was supposed to be only for mail to the provinces, and of the approximately 65 balloons that were launched, only 3 were captured by the Prussians, and 2 were lost at sea. A good reason why more balloons were not shot down and captured by the Prussians is that the Prussian guns could not be trained high enough to bring the balloon down.

All mail to be sent by balloon was to be marked "PAR BALLON MONTE."

Almost all of these famous balloons had a name, not because this would help the service or would regulate the mail, but just because this was the tempo of the Parisians during this trying time. Some of the names used were: "Le Neptune," "Le Washington," "Le Jean Bart," "Le Garibaldi," "Le Normandie," "La Gironde," "La Ville d'Orleans," "Le Volta," "L'Armee de Bretagne," "Le Deliverance," "La Poste-de-Paris," "Le General Cambronne," etc.

Herewith is a thumbnail outline of the flight of the balloon "L'Archmede." This balloon left Paris at 1 A.M. on the morning of November 21, 1870, and landed at 6:45 A.M. the same morning at Castelre, Holland. There were two passengers besides the pilot, 21 pigeons and 220 kilograms of mail; it traveled over 400 kilometers.

The following illustrations are of letters and a Balloon Gazette flown out on perhaps the above named balloons.

Balloon Post, Continued

Perhaps among the first of the airmail covers, this folded letter is postmarked **22 Sept. 1870**, during the Siege of Paris, Franco-Prussian War of 1870-1871. The receiving postmark is 18 October, at Abbeville, France. According to the dates of the cancellations, the balloon could have been *Le Neptune*, the first balloon out of Paris.

This cover was flown on the Balloon "Le General Renault," flight #42 on December 11, 1870.

Balloon Post, Continued

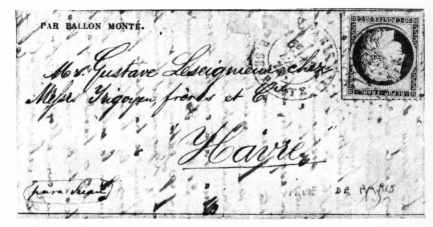

This cover is postmarked 13 December, 1870, and according to records it was probably on the balloon "LA VILLE de PARIS" which was captured by the Prussian soldiers near Wertzlur, Prussia, at about 11 A.M. of the same day of ascent, December 15, 1870.

A folded Gazette of specially prepared chronicle of events within Paris during the Siege. This could have been carried on the balloon "LE VICTOR HUGO" which ascended on October 18, 1870, at 11:45 A.M. and landed at Coeuvres near Vauberon at 5:30 P.M. of the same day.

PEACOCK OVERPRINTS
Japanese Occupation of Burma 1942

Certain stamps of Burma were overprinted with the Peacock device by the authority of the Japanese military and occupation officials as well as the Burma Independence Army. Both regular postage stamps and officials were so overprinted for postal service to indicate that the occupation authority superceded that of the Burmese government as a British Dominion.

Body and head of Peacock clearly defined by uncolored band.

Peacock has slender neck, more detailed tail. On right leg is pronounced spur.

MYAUGMYA

PYAPON

HENZADA

MYAUGMYA

HENZADA

Clear and definite strike, only type with border around peacock.

Peacock has short, straight legs, each feather is separately outlined, no curve at the base.

Clearly struck overprints show clear detail of wings and tail. Legs long and thin, claws enclose clear white space.

This type was officially applied to postal stationery only.

This type was used on King George VI official stamps.

MYAUGMYA

MYAUGMYA

INTRODUCTION TO STAMP ILLUSTRATIONS

The illustrations which follow are for the identification of postage stamps from all over the world and have been selected to show the types which are more generally found rather than to try to distinguish between such specialist categories as, for example, the A and B type papers used in the manufacture of certain early stamps of Scandinavian countries.

The selection of the material illustrated was necessarily controlled by the size of this book, but it is hoped that this really grand array of well over 3,000 philatelic illustrations will do more than identify a given stamp; let them also whet the appetite of the collector to study his or her stamps and covers and to get into the stream of research on their own.

Just for the sake of openers, we should journey back to the days long before postage stamps, to the era of the London Penny Post. It was in about 1680 when the first announcement of the new and improved scheme for mail and packet delivery was made to the people of London. The scheme was for a London Penny Post and was put into effect by William Dockwra whose idea was for people to leave their letters and packets at receiving houses or in receptacles in places of business from which they would be collected by Dockwra's messengers and taken to sorting houses for sorting and then delivered at a cost of 1 penny each letter or packet.

The following illustrations depict some of the markers applied to letters and packets to indicate time of collection, location of the point from which delivery was undertaken, etc.

Payd Peny
Post 1683

Peny Post
Payd 1689

Payd Peny
Post 1711

Abu Dhabi
Br. Protectorate

Abyssinia
(See Ethiopia)

Aden
Br. Colony

Aden, Seiyun State
Br. Protectorate

Aden
Shihr & Mukalla
Br. Protectorate

Aden
Hadhramaut
Br. Protectorate

Afghanistan, Kingdom

Afghanistan,
Kingdom

Aguera,
Spanish Colony

Aitutaki
N. Z. Dependency

Ajman
Br. Protectorate

Alaouites,
French Mandate

Albania,
Republic

Albania, Kingdom

Albania, Italian
Occupation

Albania,
Peoples' Republic

Alexandretta, French Mandate　　　Algeria, Fr. Colony

Algeria, Cable Toll Stamp　　　Algeria EA overprint for Etat
Algerien, meaning Independent State

Allenstein Plebiscite, Overprints　　Allied Military Government

Allied Military Government　　　Alsace, German Occupation
Stamp Issues (See Trieste)　　　1870　　　　　　　　1940

Alwar　　　　　　　Anatolia, Turkish Ter-
Indian State　　　　ritory in Asia Minor

Ancachs, Chilean Occ. of Peru　　Andorra, Spanish Administration

Andorra

Andorra, French Administration

Angola, Port. Colony

Angra
Azores District

Anjouan
Fr. Colony

Annam-Tonkin
Fr. Protectorate

Antigua
Br. Colony

Antioquia
Colombian State

A.O. on Belgian Congo, Belgian
Occ. German East Africa

A O F on France
Fr. West Africa

Arabia Hejaz Kingdom   Arabia Nejd Kingdom

Arequipa
Chilean Occ. Peru

Argentine
Confederation

Argentine
Republic

Armenia
National Republic

Armenia, Soviet Socialist Republic

— 43 —

Ascension Is.
Br. Colony

Australia Commonwealth
Dominion of Br. Commonwealth

Australia
Occ. Japan

Austrian
Monarchy

Austrian
Empire

Austria
Birthday Jubilee

Austrian Republic before World War II

Austria, overprints for use in Russian
protected zones after capture, 1945

Austria
Present Republic

Austria Empire
Newspaper stamps

Newspaper Tax

Austria Republic
Newspaper stamp

Austria Empire
Offices in Crete

Austria Empire, Offices in Turkey

Austria, Allied
Military Govt.

Postage Due

Austria Military Postage World War I

gray green   magenta   blue

Military
Newspaper

Special Handling

Austria Empire
Occupation Serbia WWI

Austria Empire, Italian Occupation WWI

Austria Empire, Occupation of Italy

Austria Empire, Occupation of Montenegro

Austria Empire, Occupation of Romania

Austria Empire
Danube Riverboat Post

National Republic | Soviet Socialist Republic | Baku Province | Azores Islands

Azerbaijan

B Overprint
for Bangkok

Baden
German State

Bahamas
Br. Colony

Bahawalpur
Pakistani State

Official

Bahrain Br. Protected
Sultanate

Bamra
Indian State

Barbados
Br. Colony

Barbados
Relief Fund

Barbuda, Antigua
Dependency

Barwani
Indian State

Basutoland
Br. Colony

Basutoland
(See Lesotho)

Batum
Br. Occupation

— 47 —

Bavaria
Kingdom

Bavaria
Tete Beche Pair

Bavaria
Republic

Bavaria
Republic

Bavaria Kingdom
Postage Due

Bavaria
Official

Bechuanaland
Br. Protectorate

Belgian Congo
(See Congo)

Belgian E. Africa
(See Rwanda Rep. and Kingdom of Burundi)

Belgian Occupation
of German E. Africa, WWI

Belgium

Semi Postal

Under German Occupation
World War I

Postage Due

B in circle
Official

Newspaper   Parcel Post, Railway

Parcel Post, Railway
Belgium

Benadir
(Somalia)

Benghasi
Italian Offices
in Africa

Benin
Fr. Colony

Bergedorf
German State

Bermuda
Br. Colony

Bhopal
Indian State

Bhor
Indian State

Bhutan

Bijawar
Indian State

Bogota
Colombian State

Bohemia-Moravia (Czechoslovakia)
German Protectorate during WWII

Bolivar
Colombian State

This cover was mailed February 28, 1900, during the Siege of Ladysmith in Natal during the Boer War. Stamps were not available or obtainable as the Dutch forces had the city surrounded. This is another classic little bit of history.

BOER WAR

This is also known as the South African War, from October of 1899 through 1902. The Dutch Boers fought a guerilla war, and in a series of campaigns led the British on to such famous battles as the Siege of Ladysmith and the Siege of Mafeking, etc.

It only took the British a few months to realize that the Boers were more prepared for war than had been expected; and the British Army, under Lord Roberts, pushed ahead with mounted troops to eventually win the war in 1902, by the Treaty of Vereeniging.

The following illustrations depict some of the local stamps used during the trying time of siege, as well as occupation overprints and the use of British stamps in South Africa:

Siege of Mafeking

Lydenburg

Springfontien

Rustenberg

Klerksdorp

Natal

Standerton

Volkrust

Commando Label

Bolivia

gray green   brown red   violet

Archduchess Sophie and Archduke Ferdinand. Assassinated June 28, 1914, at Sarajevo, Bosnia, which precipitated World War I.

Military Postage Due   Postage Due   Newspaper

Bosnia-Herzegovina Province of Austro-Hungarian Empire

Boyaca Colombian State

Bremen
German State

Imperial Brazil
Bull's Eye

Dom Pedro
Emperor of Brazil

Republic

Br. Antarctic
Territory

British Central
Africa

British
Colombia

British East
Africa Co.

British East
Africa Protectorate

British Guiana

British Honduras

Eritrea

E. Africa

Malaya

Somalia

British Military
Authority

Sarawak

Tripolitania

Burma

British Military Postal Label
EGYPT

British New
Guinea

British Solomon
Islands

Br. Somaliland   Brunei

Brunei, Japanese
Occupation WWII

Brunswick
German State

Buenos Aires
Argentina

Bulgaria as
Turkish Protectorate

Bulgaria Kingdom

Bulgaria
Peoples Republic

Official

Bulgaria
Parcel Post

Bulgaria
Flood Relief

Bulgaria   Republic
Imperial Postage Due

Postal Tax

Bundi
Indian State

Official

Burgos, Spanish Civil War

Burma as
British Prot.

Burma
Military Govt.

Burma
Interim Govt.

Burma
Republic

Japanese Occu-
pation WWII

Burma Peacock
Overprint

Burma, the
Yano Seal

Burma, Japanese
Stamp surcharged
during WWII

Japanese Occupation WWII

Burundi Kingdom
(See Belg. E. Africa)

Bushire, Br. Occupation
Persian Port, WWI

Bussahir
Indian State

Cabo Gracias A Dios
District of Nicaragua

Calchi (Karki)   Calino
Italian Aegean Is.

Callao, Chilean
Occupation Peru

Cambodia

Cameroon
German Colony

Cameroon under French Occupation WWI

Cameroon under
British
Occupation WWI

Cameroon as a
French Colony

Cameroon as a
Republic

Canada
Province

Canada
Dominion

Canal Zone

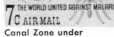

Canal Zone under
U.S. jurisdiction

Canary Islands
(See Spanish Civil War)

Cape of Good Hope

Cape of Good
Hope, Vryburg
Issue under Boer
Occupation

Cape of Good
Hope, Siege of
Mafeking

Cover from Siege of Mafeking
Boer War

Cape Juby
Spanish Colony

Cape Verde
Port. Colony

Austria
Carinthia Plebiscite

Jugoslavia

Caroline Isalnds
German Colony

Carpatho-Ukraine

**Caso-Italian
Aegean Is.**

**Base
Navale Francais**

**Occupation
Navale Francais**

Italian Dominion Castellorizo

Cauca Colombian Distr.

**Cavalle
Fr. Offices Turkey**

**Cavalla
Greek Occupation**

**Cayman Islands
Br. Colony**

**Celebes Islands
Japanese Naval
Occupation WWII**

Central African Republic

Central Lithuania

Ceylon as British Colony

Ceylon

Ceylon as Republic

Chachapoyas, Chilean Occupation Peru

Chad as French Colony

Chad as Republic

Chamba
Indian State

Charkhari
Indian State

Chee Foo
China Local Post

Chiclayo, Chilean
Occupation Peru

Chile

The following types of overprints were used on provisional issues during the War of the Pacific between Chile and Peru, 1879-1882:

Type of cancellation denoting, by city and date, occupation of Peru by Chile

General occupation issues of Chile during occupation of Peru.

China Imperial Postage

Foochow, 1912
Provisional

Nanking, 1912
Provisional

Issues of the Republic

   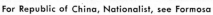

For Republic of China, Nationalist, see Formosa

China, Offices
in Tibet, 1911

Chios
Greek Occ

Christmas Is.
Terr. of Australia

Cilicia, 1919
French Occupation

Cilicia, 1920 French Occupation

Coamo Puerto Rico Emergency

Cochin China
French Colony

Cochin
Indian State

Cocos & Keeling Is.
Terr. of Australia

Granadine
Confederation

New Granada
Colombia

United States of
Colombia

Colombia Republic

Colombia

Colombia Airmail

Colombia
Scadta Issue

Airmail

Garzon Postmaster
Provisional
Air Mail

Comoro Islands
French Overseas
Poss.

Congo Republic
(Belgian Congo)

Congo Republic
(Fr. Middle Congo)

Coo, Italian
Aegean Is.

Corrientes
Argentine Province

Council of Europe

Cook Islands, New Zealand Dependency comprises Rarotonga, Aitutaki, Penrhyn Is., etc.

Corfu Island (Greek)
Italian Occupation 1923

1941 Issue for Corfu and Paxo
under Italian Occupation

Costa Rica

Costa Rica
Guanacaste Province

Crete, British
Administration

Crete, Russian
Sphere of Influence

Crete, National
Government

Crete
Postage Due

Crete
Official

Croatia State
1941-1945

Croatia-Slavonia
Provinces of Jugoslav Kingdom
1918-1919

Cuba and Puerto Rico
Spanish Dominion

Cuba Only

Cuba

Cuba, U.S.
Administration

Cuba, under
U.S. Military

Cuba Republic

Cuba, Matanzas
Zone

Cundinamarca, Colombian State

Curacao, see
Netherlands Antilles

Curacao,
Postage Due,
green

Cuzco, Chilean
Occupation Peru

Cyprus as a
British Colony

Republic of Cyprus

Cyprus as a
Republic

Cyrenaica as
Italian Colony

Czechoslovakia
First Republic

Czechoslovakia
People's Republic

Czechoslovakia
overprint on Austria

Czechoslovakia
Postage Due

Czechoslovakia
Siberian Legion

Bohemia-Moravia

Under German Protectorate WWII
Czechoslovakia

Slovakia

Dagistan
Republic

Dahomey
Fr. Colony

Dahomey
Republic

Dalmatia
Italian Occ.
1921-1922

Value in
cents

For frame
varieties
see page 12

Danish West Indies

Danzig Overprint
on Germany

Danzig, Free Port City
Postage Due

Official

Dedeagh, French
Offices Turkey

Denmark
skilling values

For detailed draw-
ings and explana-
tions of the normal
and the inverted
frame lines of this
design, see page 12.

Late Fee

Postage Due

Military

Official

Parcel Post

Danish Faroe
Islands, German
Occupation 1940

Danish Faroe
Islands, British
Occ. 1940-41

Dhar
Indian State

Diego Suarez
French Colony

Djibouti (Somali Coast Port City) French Possession

Dominica
Br. Colony

Dominican Republic

Double
Print

Dubai, British
Protected Sheikdom

Durazzo, Italian
Offices in Turkey

Dutch East Indies (See also Indonesia)

Postage Due
carmine

Official

Dutch East Indies
Japanese Occupation WWII

Dutch New
Guinea

Duttia
India State

E. Africa and
Uganda
British Colony

East India
Company
(See India)

Eastern Roumelia under
Turkish Empire. (See
South Bulgaria)

Eastern Silesia
Plebiscite Issue

Ecuador Republic

Ecuador Republic

Postage Due

Galapagos Islands
Province of Ecuador

Egypt, as part of
Turkish Empire

Egypt, as British
Protectorate

Egypt, as
Kingdom

Egypt, as Republic

Egypt, as part of
United Arab Republic

Egypt, British
Military stamp

Egypt, Occupation
of Palestine

Elobey, Annobon
and Corisco
Spanish Colony

Epirus Chimarra Issue 1914

Epirus Provisional Govt.

Epirus Greek
Occ. 1914-16

Epirus
Greek Occ. WWI

Epirus (North)
Greek Occ. WWII

Eritrea
Italian Colony

Estonia Republic

German Occ. WWI

Ethiopia (Abyssinia)

Airmail
Ethiopia

Postage Due

Ethiopia, Italian
Occupation 1936

Eupen and Malmedy Belgian occupation of the German Districts of Eupen
and Malmedy during WWI. (See Malmedy)

Falkland Is.
Br. Colony

Falkland Is. Dep.
Br. Colony

Far Eastern Republic

Far Eastern Republic
Gen. Semenov Occupation

Faridkot
Indian State

Federated Malay
States
Br. Protectorate

Federation of
Malaya, British
Commonwealth

Fernando Po
Spanish Colony

Fezzan-Ghadames
(Kingdom of Libia)

Fezzan (See
Ghadames)

Fiji Islands
British Colony

Finland

As a Grand Duchy of Imperial Russia

As a Republic

Finland
Military postage

Finland, Occupa-
tion of Russia, 1919

Comparison of Finnish and Russian Stamps Issued while Finland was a Grand Duchy under Imperial Russia.

Note Circles

Finland   Russia   Finland   Russia

Finland   Russia   Finland   Russia

Fiume
1918-1924

Foochow
China Local Post

Formosa

Formosa, Chinese Nationalist Republic on Taiwan Island.

France
2nd Republic 1848

France
2nd Empire 1852

France
3rd Republic 1871-

France, Vichy Government
German Occupation WWII

France

Postage Due

Military

Council of Europe
(Official Mail from
Strasbourg)

France, (German
Occup. Alsace-
Lorraine) 1870

France, (German
Occupation WWI)

Alsace

Lorraine

France, (German Occup. of Alsace-Lorraine WWII)

France, Allied Military
Government, 1944-1945

Postage Due

French Post Offices Abroad
General Issues, China

Canton

Hoi Hao

Kwangchowan

Mongtseu

Pakhoi

Tchongking

Yunnan Fou

Crete

Egypt

Turkey,
General

Turkey, General

Cavalle, Turkey

Dedeagh,
Turkey

Port Lagos, Turkey

Vathy, Turkey

Zanzibar

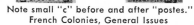
Note small "c" before and after "postes."
French Colonies, General Issues

French Colonies, General Issues

French Congo

French Equatorial Africa

French Equatorial Africa

French Guiana

French Guinea

French India   Free French

French Indo China, prior to political division into Laos, Cambodia, Viet Nam.

French Indo China
Postage Due

(For use in Annam)

(For use in Cambodia)

French Morocco

For use in city of Tangier

French Morocco Postage Due

French Morocco Parcel Post

French Oceania (Polynesia)

Free French

French Polynesia

French South and Antarctic Territories

French Soudan

French W. Africa

French W. Africa

Fujeira, Br. Protected Sheikdom

Funchal, Port. Colony

Gabon, Fr. Colony

Gabon Republic

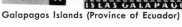

Galapagos Islands (Province of Ecuador)

Gambia, Br. Colony

Gambia as a State of Br. Commonwealth

General Government
(German Occupied Poland, WWII)

Georgia as part of
Soviet Socialist Rep.

Georgia
National Republic

Pesa currency

Heller currency

German E. Africa, German Colony

Belgian Occupation   1918   British Occupation   1917
1916   1916
             German E. Africa, German Colony

German New Guinea
German Colony

German New Guinea under
occupation by British land
and sea forces, 1914-1915,
and known as New Britain.

Hyphen Bet.
"Sudwest" and "Afrika"

No Hyphen
German S.W. Africa
German Colony

Germany as
Empire

Germany as
Republic

Germany as
Third Reich

Germany under U.S.
and British control

Germany
Federal Republic

Germany
Berlin

Germany
Airmail

Germany
Military

Germany
Official

Allemagne, Germany,
Belg. Occ. WWI

Germany
Inselpost (Crete)

Germany, Submarine
stamp for mail from
Hela Province

Germany, Allied
Military Government

General   **Baden**   Germany, French Occupation 1945   **Rheinland-Pfalz**   **Wurttemberg**

Germany, Berlin—Allied Sector

Germany, Berlin—Russian Sector

German Democratic Republic—(East Germany)

Germany, Imperial Offices Abroad, 1884-1913
China

Morocco

Turkey

Ghadames
(See Fezzan-
Ghadames)

Ghana

Gibraltar
Br. Colony

Gilbert and Ellice Is.—British Colony

Gold Coast
Br. Colony

Graham Land (Falkland
Dependency, British Colony)

Grand Comoro Is.
Fr. Colony

GREAT BRITAIN
THE WORLD'S FIRST POSTAGE STAMP
May 6, 1840

A most fascinating and intriguing part of stamp collecting is the discovery of where a given stamp was used, especially in such a far-flung and hard fought-for empire as that of the early British Empire. With creditable foresight and diligent planning, the post office assigned letters and numbers to a colony or protectorate territory or foreign office so that the cancellations on the stamps of the mother country used in these areas could be identified as to the point of origin. The following illustrations depict various British stamps used abroad.

Constantinople
1876-1879

St. Thomas,
1876, Danish
W. Indies

Malta
1867

Panama, 1877
Colombia

Gibraltar
1865

Kung-Chow
China

Puerto Plata,
Dom. Rep.
1862-69

Suez, Egypt
1873-77

Used in South
Africa during Boer
War. Army post
office "B" at
Bloemfontien,
March 10, 1902.

Internal
Revenue

Govt.
Parcels

Office of
Works

Army

Royal
Household

Board of
Education

Admiralty

Middle East
Military Forces

Eritrea, Br. Occ.
Italian Colony

East Africa Forces, Br. Occupation
Somalia, former Italian Colony

Tripolitania, Br.
Occ. Italian Colony

Tripolitania

Offices in
China

Offices in Morocco using
Spanish currency

Offices in Morocco using
French currency

Offices in Morocco using
British currency

Great Britain
Offices in Tangier

Great Britain
Offices in Turkey

Great Britain
Offices in Turkey

Greece as kingdom

Greece, under Provisional Govt.

Greece as
Republic

Greece under the
restored monarchy

King Constantine and
Queen Anne-Marie (a
former princess of Denmark)

Greece
Airmail

Greece
Postage Due

Greece Postage Due

Greece Postal Tax

Greenland
Danish Col.

Grenada
Br. Colony

Griqualand W.
Br. Colony

Grodno
So. Lithuania

Guadeloupe
Fr. Colony

Guadeloupe Fr. Colony

Postage Due

Guam, under U.S. Admin.

Guanacaste
(Costa Rica Prov.)

Guatemala

Guayana
(Venezuela Distr.)

Guinea Rep.

Guyana Republic
(Formerly Br.
Guiana)

Gwalior Indian State

Haiti

Hamburg
German States

Hanover

Haucho (Chile Occ. Peru)

Hawaii
Missionary

Kingdom of Hawaii

Provisional Govt.

Hawaii Republic

Hatay, (See
Alexandretta)

Heligoland
Br. Possession

Holkar
Indian State

Danish
Holstein
Province

Prussian

Honduras

Honduras
Reprint Cancel

Honduras

Honduras, showing
accounting control mark

Hong Kong
Br. Colony

Japanese
Occup. WWII

Horta Port. Colony   Hungary, as part of the Austro-Hungarian Empire

Hungary, as a
democratic republic

Hungary, as a
soviet republic

Hungary, anti-
soviet govt.

Hungary, Banat
district issue

Hungary, as a
kingdom under
regency of
Adm. Horthy

Hungary
Airmail

Hungary, Danube
River Packet Mail

Hungary, showing
Crown of
St. Stephen

French Occ.

Serbian Occ.

Romanian Occ.

1st Debrecen

After World War II Hungary declared itself a "People's Republic" under the "protection" of Soviet Russia. A wild inflation took place and is reflected by the values of the postage stamps:

In an attempt to control the aftereffects of inflation and stabilize the use of postage stamps, many different overprints of words or abbreviations were applied to existing stamps to designate a postal category. Some basic varieties are shown here:

Local letter:
Hl. I or with:
Helyi level

Parcel post: Cs. 5-1.
or with:
Csomag 10 kg.

Registration
Ajl. 2.

Domestic letter:
Tl. I. or with:
Tavolsagi level

Domestic postcard:
Tip-2. or with:
Tavolsagi lev-lap

Printed matter:
Any. 1. or with:
Nyomtatv

Local postcard:
Hlp. or with:
Helyi lev.-lap

Printed Matter
Any. 1.

Parcel Post
Csomag 10 kg.

Hyderabad
Indian State

Icaria
Gr. Occup.

Iceland

Idar,
Indian State

Ifni, Spanish Colony

India, as part
of British Empire

India, as a Republic

INDIA

The fame of the great fighting qualities of the trained Indian soldier is known the world over. Many times have contingents of Indian troops served brilliantly and with distinction with other forces in widely separated parts of the world. The following are some of the stamp designs and overprints which were for the use of the Indian troops abroad:

Chinese
Expeditionary
Force (Boxer
Rebellion)

Indian
Expeditionary
Force (World
War I)

Korea Custodial
Force

Congo, United
Nations Force

Ghaza Strip,
United Nations
Force

Cambodia Force

Laos Force

Laos & Viet Nam
Force

Viet Nam

Indian Native Feudatory States

The following illustrations depict some basic postage stamp designs
as used by the feudatory states of India, which had franking power only
within the states in which they were issued. Travancore and Cochin
being the only exceptions.

Alwar

Bamra

Barwani

Bhopal

Bhor

Bijawar

Bundi

Bussahir

Charkhari

Cochin

Dhar

Duttia

Faridkot

Holkar

Holkar

Hyderabad

Idar

Indore

Jaipur

Jammu   Jammu & Kashmir

Jasdan

Jhalawar

Jhind

Kishanagarh

Las Bela

Morvi

Nandgaon

Nowanugger

Orchha

Poonch

Rajasthan

Rajpeepla

Sirmoor

Soruth

Travancore

Wadhwan

Japanese
stamp ovpt.

Dutch Indies
stamp ovpt.

Japanese occupa-
tion stamp over-
printed

United States
of Indonesia

(See Riau
Archipelago)

Indonesia Provisionals

Postage Due

Indore
Indian State

Inhambane
Port. Colony

Inini
Fr. Colony

Inner Mongolia
Japanese Occupation

International Court
of Justice,
Netherlands

Ionian Islands
Br. Protectorate

Ionian Islands
Italian Occ. 1941

Ionian Islands
German Occ. 1943

For issues of Iran (Persia) prior to 1935 when the country name
was changed, see "Persia."

Iraq, Br. Mandate   Rupee currency   Iraq Kingdom   Iraq Republic

Ireland
Provisional Govt.

Ireland
Republic

Ireland
Postage Due

Israel

Istria
(Post WWII issues)

Italian Colonies
General issues

Italian
East Africa

Postage Due

Italian Somaliland

Italy as Kingdom

Parcel Post

Official

Postage Due   Authorized Delivery   Pneumatic Post   Military

1946
ITALY AS REPUBLIC

Italian Social
Republic, 1944

U.S. and British
Occupation Zones

Allied Military
Government
District of Venezia
Giulia

Italy Kingdom
with fasces

Italy Kingdom
without fasces

Italian Office Abroad

General Issues

Peking
China

Tientsin
China

Crete

Africa
Benghasi

Tripoli

General Issues

Albania

Constantinople

Durazzo

Janina

Jerusalem

Salonika

Scutari

Smyrna

Valona

Turkish Empire

General Issues

Calchi

Calino

Caso

Coo

Lero

Lisso

Nisiro

Patmo

Piscopi

Rhodes

Scarpanto

Simi

Stampalia

Aegean Islands, Italian Occupation

Ivory Coast

Ivory Coast
French Colony

Parcel
Post

Ivory Coast
Republic

Jaipur
Indian State

Jamaica
Br. Colony

Jamaica
Independent State

Jammu
Indian State

Jammu and Kashmir
Indian States

Japan

Military

Offices in
China

Offices in
Korea

Offices in
Formosa

Jasdan
Indian State

Jhalawar
Indian State

Jhind
Indian State

Japanese Occ.
Johore State

Johore State
British Prot.

Jordan Br. Mandate

Jordan Br. Mandate

Jordan Kingdom

Juan Fernandez Is.
Province of Chile

Jugoslavia—Bosnian stamps surcharged and overprinted
for use in Bosnia-Herzegovina District of Kingdom of
Jugoslavia, 1918.

Jugoslavia—Stamps for use in Croatia-Slavonia
Dis. of Kingdom of Jugoslavia, 1918.

Jugoslavia—Stamps for use in
the Slovenia District of the
Kingdom of Jugoslavia, 1918.

Jugoslavia
Carinthia
Plebiscite

Jugoslavia Kingdom

Bi-Lingual Pair

Postage Due

Jugoslavia, Imperial
Govt. in Exile, London, 1943.

Jugoslavia People's Republic, 1944-

German Occupation
Jugoslavia WWII

Allied Occupation of the
Slovenian Coast and
Istria, WWII

Military Government of Trieste

Karelia
Republic, 1922

Karelia, Finnish
Occupation 1941-42

Kashmir
Indian State

Kedah
Br. Prot.

Kedah as
Malay State

Kedah
Japanese Occ.

Kelantan as Malay State

Kelantan
Japanese Occ.

Kenya, Uganda and Tanganyika
British Colony

Kenya, Uganda
and Tanzania

Kenya Republic

Kewkiang
China Local Post

Khor Fakkan
Br. Protected Sheikdom

Kiauchau
German Colony

Kionga
Port. Colony

Kishangarh, Indian State

Korea as Kingdom

Korea, U.S. Military
on Japanese stamps

Korea as
Republic

Kuwait as British
Protected Sheikdom

Kuwait as British
Protected State

Labuan, Br. Colony

Lagos
Br. Colony

Laos Kingdom

Las Bela
Indian State

Latakia
Fr. Mandate

Republic of Latvia
The first stamps of Latvia were printed on the backs of some
German WWI military maps.

Stamps printed on the backs of unfinished Communist bank notes, 1919.

Latvia
German Occ. WWI

Latvia
German Occ. WWII

Latvia
Russian Occ. 1919

League of Nations
Switzerland

Lebanon under
French Mandate

Lebanon
Republic

Lebanon Inde-
pendent Republic

Lebanon
Postal Tax

Leeward Is.
Br. Colony

Lemnos, Greek
Occupation 1912

Lero Italian
Occupation
1912-1943

Lesotho, formerly
British Basutoland

Liberia Republic

Liberia,
Registration

Libia,
as Italian possession

Kingdom of   Fezzan
Libya (Libia)

French Occupation of Italian Libia, 1946-51

Swiss Administration, 1921-

Liechtenstein
Austrian Administration, 1912-1918

Lisso, Aegean Is.
Italian Occupation 1912-43

Thick   1st Kaunas   2nd Kaunas   3rd Kaunas
Figures   Printing   Printing   Printing

German Occupation   Russian Occupation
World War I   1940

Lithuania

R.Commissariato
Civile
Territori Sloveni
occupati
LUBIANA

Italian   German   Lombardy-Venetia
Occupation   Occupation   as part of Austro-Hungarian Empire
Ljubljana (Jugoslavia Distr.)

Lourenco Marques, Port. Colony   Half of Large Stamp   German State
                                                         Lubeck

Grand Duchy of Luxembourg

 (top right) *Perforated Official*

German Occupation WWII

Grand Duchy of Luxembourg

Perforated Official

Macao, Portuguese Colony

Macao
War Tax

Madagascar
French Colony

Madagascar
British Consular Mail, 1884-6

Vichy Govt.

Madagascar
Free French

Madeira
Port. Colony

Malacca
Malay State

Malacca
Japanese Occupation
WWII, hand stamped for
use in all Malacca area

Malagasy
Republic (see
Madagascar)

Malaya

Mali Federation

Mali Republic
Mali (formerly French Sudan)

Malaysia Federation

Malawi State
(formerly Br. Nyasaland)

Malmedy Dist.
Belgian Occ. WW1

Maldive Islands
British Protectorate

Maldive Islands
Independent Sultanate

Malta

Malta
British Colony

Manchukuo
5 characters
across top
1932

Manchukuo
6 characters
across top
1934-36

Airmail

Local Ovpt.
End of War

Manchukuo, Japanese Puppet State

Manchuria
Chinese stps. ovpt.
for use in Kirin and
Heilungkiang Provinces

Marianna
Islands
Spanish Colony

German Colony

Marienwerder
Plebescite Issue

Marshall Islands
German Colony

Martinique (now part of French Republic) as a French Colony

Mauritania
French Colony

Islamic Republic

Mayotte
French Colony

Mauritius, British Colony

Mecklenburg Schwerin
German State

Mecklenburg-
Strelitz

Memel
Commission Govt.

Memel
Lithuanian Occ. 1923-24

Meng
Chiang
Jap. Occ. China

Middle Congo
as French Colony

Baghdad Issue

Iraq Issue

Mosul Issue

British Occupation of Mesopotamia

Mexico Republic   Empire 1864   Republic

Republic   Sonora   Oaxaca   Baja Calif.

Civil War Issue 1913-14

Provisional   Sinaloa   Yucatan   Porte de Mar
Guadalajara   Revolutionary   Revolutionary   Foreign mail,
                                                             Captain's fee

Modena   Moheli   Moldavia   Moldavia-
Italian State   Fr. Colony   Romanian State   Wallachia
                                                             Romanian
                                                             State

Principality of Monaco

Mongolia

Montenegro
Kingdom

Mongolia Republic

Montenegro Kingdom

Montenegro
Kingdom

Postage Due

Austrian
Occ. 1917

Italian
Occ. 1941

German
Occ. 1943

Montserrat

Moquegua
Chile Occ. Peru

Morocco
Kingdom

Morvi
Indian State

Mozambique
Portuguese Colony

Mozambique
Postage Due

Mozambique Company
Portuguese Charter

Muscat and Oman
Br. Prot. Sultanate

SOME TYPES AND DESIGNS
OF MOURNING STAMPS

In days gone by it was customary to use a black bordered envelope when writing to friends and relatives to tell them of a death. Some nations followed this custom by issuing stamps with a black border as an international indication of national mourning when a great person had passed on. Mourning stamps should not be confused with commemorative stamps issued in honor of, or in commemoration of an anniversary of death printed in colors.

Belgium Congo
King Albert

United States
Pres. Harding

Belgium
Queen Astrid

Poland
Marshal Pilsudski

Germany
Pres. Hindenburg

Greece
King George II

Austria
Chancellor Dollfuss

Finland
Jean Sibelius

Jugoslavia
King Alexander

Hungary
Stephen Horthy

Israel
Chaim Weizmann

Nabha
Indian State

Nandgaon
Indian State

Naples
Italian State

Natal Br. Colony

Nauru Australian Trusteeship

Negri Sembilan State, Malaya

Japanese Occ. WWII

Kingdom of Nepal

Postage Due, blue

Kingdom of the Netherlands

German Occ. WWII

International Court
of Justice, based
at The Hague,
Netherlands

Netherlands Antilles
(see Curacao)

Nevis
Br. Colony

New Britain
(Br. Occ. Ger.
NG. WWI)

New Brunswick
Br. Prov., Canada

New Caledonia Free French

New Caledonia (French Territory Overseas)

Newfoundland (now part of Canada)

United States of
New Granada
(Colombia)

New Guinea
Australian
Mandate

British
New Hebrides Islands
Condominium Govt.

French

New Hebrides Islands   New Republic South Africa

New South Wales Australian State   New Zealand

Life Insurance
Dominion of New Zealand, British Commonwealth

— 118 —

N.F. overprinted
on Nyasaland
"Nyasaland Forces"
for Br. Occ. of
Ger. E. Af.

Nicaragua

Zelaya Province

Cabo Gracias a Dios Distr.

Republic of Nicaragua

Niger Coast
Br. Prot.

Niger Terr.
French Colony

French Colony
Vichy Govt.

Republic

Nigeria
Br. Colony

Republic

Niue Islands
Dep. of New Zealand

Norfolk Islands
Dep. Austraila

North Borneo British Colony

North Borneo
Japanese Occ.
WWII

North China
Japanese Occ.
WWII

North Epirus
Greek Occ. of
Albania

Northern Nigeria
British Colony

Northern Rhodesia

No. German Postal
Confederation

No. Ingermanland
Provisional Govt.

Official Stamps

Nazi Emblem
Kingdom of Norway

N.W. Pacific Islands
Australian Military
Govt. for Nauru
and part of Ger-
man New Guinea

Nossi-Be
Fr. Protectorate

Nova Scotia
(now part of
Canada)

Nowanuggur (Navanager) Indian State

Nyassaland British Protectorate

Nyassaland Br. Prot. (now Malawi)

Nyassa Port. Colony

Nyassa

Obock
Fr. Somaliland Port

Oil Rivers
Br. Prot. on Niger
Coast

Oldenburg
German
State

Oltre Guiba
Ital. Colony

Orange
Free State
as a Republic

Orange Free
State Br. Occ.
Boer War

Orange Free
State as
British Colony

Orcha
Indian State

Pahang
Malay State

Japanese Occ.
WWII

Paita
Chile Occ. Peru

Pakistani Republic

Palestine, British Mandate

Panama (Colombian Dominion)

Panama City Issue

Panama Colon Issue

Republic of Panama

Papua, first known as British New Guinea

Papua

Papua-New Guinea
(1952)

Republic of Paraguay

Parma
Ital. State

Pasco

Patiala
Indian State

Patmo
Ital. Occ.
Aegean Is.

Penang
Malay State

Penrhyn Islands
Dep., New Zealand

Perak, Malay State

Japanese Occ.
WWII

Perlis, Malay State

Persia

Persia

Parcel Post   **Airmail**   **Official**

Kingdom of Persia (Iran)   Name Changed to Iran

Republic of Peru

Republic of Peru

Republic of Peru   **Postage Due**

Peru
Parcel Post

Postal Tax

Philippine Is.
Spanish Admin.

American Dominion

Commonwealth

Japanese
Occ. WWII

Victory Ovpt.

Republic

Pigeon Post—Used between Great Barrier Is. and Auckland, New Zealand

Pisco
Chile Occ.
Peru

Piscopi
Ital. Occ. Aegean Is.

Pitcairn Is.
Br. Colony

Piura
Chile Occ.
Peru

Poland as Kingdom
under Russia 1860

Poland as a
Republic 1918

German stamps overprinted
and surcharged for the Polish
Republic, 1918-1919.

Austrian military stamps overprinted
and surcharged for use as Polish
Republic; Lublin issue, 1918-1919.

Cracow Issue
1919

Austrian stamp
overprinted for use
as Polish Republic;
Cracow issue, 1919.

German stamps overprinted and
surcharged for POZNAN or POSEN
district, 1919.

Northern Poland

Southern Poland

Pre-World War I

Republic

People's Republic

German Occupation
World War I
Poland

German
Occ. WWII

General Gov. German Occ. WWII   Offices in Danzig   Offices in Turkey

Poland, Government in Exile, 1941-44.

Ponta Delgada
Port. Colony

Poonch
Indian State

Port Lagos
Fr. Off. Turkey

Portugal as Kingdom   Portugal as Republic

Portugal
Postage Due

Postal Tax

Portugal
Military

Portugal
War Tax

Portugal
Parcel Post

Portugal
Postal Tax Due

Portugal
Red Cross

Portugal
Newspaper

**Portuguese
Africa**

**Portuguese
Congo**

**Port. Congo
Newspaper**

Portuguese Guinea

Postage Due

**Portuguese Guinea
Postal Tax**

Portuguese India

Portuguese India

**Pr. Edw. Island
(now part of
Canada)**

Prussia, German State

Puerto Rico, Spanish Dominion

Coamo
Puerto Rico American Dominion

Puno, Chile Occ. Peru

Qatar   Queensland   Quelimane
Br. Prot. Sheikdom   Australian State   Port. Colony

Rajasthan, Indian State   Rajpeepla, Indian State

Rarotonga Dep. New Zealand   Ras Al Khaima Br. Protected Sheikdom

Reunion Is., Former French Colony

Rheinland-Pfalz
Allied Occ.
Germany

Rhodes
Ital. Occ.
Aegean Is.

Rhodesia
Under Br. So.
Af. Co. Admin.

Rhodesia, Self-governing
State (Formerly Southern
Rhodesia)

Rhodesia

Rhodesia and
Nyasaland as
part of Federation

Riau-Lingga
Archipelago
(Indo. Admin.)

Rio de Oro
Spanish Colony

Rio Muni
Spanish Colony

Romagna
Italian State

Roman States

Principality of
Moldavia, Romania

Principality
of Moldavia-Wallachia

Unissued
design

Kingdom of Romania

Romania
People's Republic

Romania
Postage due

Romania
Parcel Post

Romania
Postal tax

Romania
Off. in Turkey

Romania, under
Austrian Occ. WWI

Romania, Under
Bulgarian Occ.
WW1

Romania, under
German Occ. WW1

Romania, under German
Occupation WWI

Ross Dependency
(New Zealand)

Rouad Is. Fr. Colony

Ruanda-Urundi (Belg. E. Africa)

Imperial Russia

Provisional Govt.
after revolution, 1917

Russian Socialist
Federal Soviet Republic

Russia, stamps printed on thick paper for use as currency;
imprinted on back.

Russia, Army of
NW. Gen. Yudenich

Russia, Union of Soviet Republics, 1923-

Russia, Charity
issue, 1914

Russia
Postage due

Russia
Postal savings

Russia
Special delivery

Russia
Wenden Distr. of Livonia
Province of Russian Empire

Russia Finnish
Occupation
of Russia, 1919

Russia
German Occ. 1941-3

Army of the North
Gen. Yudenich

Army of Gen.
Miller
(not issued)

Russian Offices
in Crete

Russia, Occupation
Germany WWII

Latvian stamp
Russia, W. Army under Col. Bermondt-Avalov, 1919.

Russian stamp

Russia, Occ.
Latvia, WWII

Russia, Occ.
Lithuania, WWII

Russia, Imperial Offices in China

Russia, Imperial Offices in Turkey

IMPERIAL RUSSIAN STAMPS
Overprinted and Surcharged by the Czarist
General Baron Peter Wrangel, 1921

One of the last units of the Imperial Russian Army is known to philatelists because of the stamps overprinted and surcharged for the use of the remnants of the Volunteer Army under the masterful leadership of General Baron Peter Wrangel.

This Volunteer Army was composed of men who preferred the imperial system of government as well as tens of thousands of refugees from the steady reign of brutality and terror of the bolshevik forces. After his defeat in the Crimea, General Wrangel and his forces retreated into Turkish territory with the help of units of the American, British and French navies.

Postal facilities were established, and various Russian stamps were overprinted "Stamps of the Russian Army" and surcharged in denominations of 1,000, 5,000, 10,000 and 20,000 rubles.

The following illustrations depict various stamps and overprints and surcharges of the Wrangel issues:

Rwanda Republic

Ryukyu Islands

Ryukyu Islands

Saar,
Fr. Protectorate

Saar

Saar, German
Admin.

St. Christopher,
Brit. Colony

St. Christopher-Nevis-
Anguilla, Br. Colony

St. Helena, Br. Colony

St. Lucia, Br. Colony

St. Marie de
Madagascar
Fr. Colony

St. Pierre & Miquelon, French Colony

St. Thomas & Prince Is.
Portuguese Colony

St. Vincent, Br. Colony

Sabah
Br. Protected
State of Malaysia

Salvador
Overprinted
with device
known as
"Catherine
Wheel"

Salvador

Salvador

Official

Samoa Kingdom

Samoa
Kingdom

Samoa
Ger. Colony

Samoa
Br. possession

Samoa
Br. Occ.
WWI

Samos Is.
Greek Occ.

Samos Is., Provisional Govt. Greek Occupation 1912-1914

Republic of San Marino   Santander, Colombian State

Santander, Colombian State   Sarawak   Sardinia
                                                  (Embossed center)
                                                  Italian State

Saseno   Saudi Arabia (See Hejaz, Nejd)   Saxony
Ital. Occ. 1923   German State

Schleswig   Schleswig, Plebiscite issues   Schleswig-Holstein
German State   German State

Selangor,
Malay State

Selangor, Japanese Occ. WWII

Senegal
Fr. Colony

Senegal
Republic

Kingdom of Serbia

Death mask design of Serbian commemorative stamp. When stamp is
turned upside-down, another face is
visible, as this enlarged and accen-
tuated illustration shows.

Serbia, Postage Due   Serbia, Austrian Occ. WWI   Serbia, German Occ. WWII

Seville issue   Seychelles Is.   Sharjah, Depend. Br. Prot. Sheikdom
(Sp. Civil War, 1936)   Brit. Colony

Shanghai local post

Siam (Thailand)

Siam (Thailand)   Siamese Occ. of
                                                             Malaya, WWII

Siberia provisional   Siberia   Siberia Czechoslovak
under Adm. Kolchak   Priamur Issue   Legion, 1919

Sierra Leone
Brit. Colony

Sierra Leone
Independent

Simi, Ital. Occ. Aegean Is.

Singapore, Br. Prot. Malaysia

Sinkiang, Prov. of China

Sirmoor, Indian State

Slovakia State, German Protec. WWII

Slovenia
State
Jugoslavia

Somalia
(See Benadir;
Ital. Somaliland)

Somali Coast
French Colony

Somali Coast
Vichy

Somali Coast
Free French

Somali Coast
Fr. Overseas Terr.

Somaliland Protectorate, British Colony

Soruth, Indian State   Union So. Africa, Bi-lingual pair

South Africa   So. Arabia Fed.   South Australia
Republic   Br. Protected   Australian State

South Bulgaria (Eastern Roumelia)   South Cameroons   So. Nigeria
                                     United Kingdom   Br. Colony
                                     Trust Territory

So. Rhodesia   So. Georgia Is.   So. Orkneys Is.
Br. Colony   Falkland Dep.   Falkland Dep.

So. Russia
Don Govt.

So. Russia
Kuban Govt.

So. Russia
Crimea

So. Russia
Volunteer Army of
General Deniken

So. Shetlands Is.
Falkland Dep.

So. Viet Nam

Ger. Col.

South West Africa
British Administration

Spain, Kingdom 1850-1869

Spain
Prov. Govt.
1868-9

Spain
Regency of
the Duke
de la Torre
1870

Spain
Kingdom
1872-77

Spain
First Republic 1873-74

Spain, Kingdom 1875-1930

Madrid printing   1st Barcelona   2nd Barcelona   General
                       printing   printing
                     Spanish Revolution Issues

Spain, Republic under General Franco

Spain   Spain, Restoration of   Spain   Spain
Red Cross   the Catacombs   Autogiro Airmail   Official

Spanish Guinea   Spanish Morocco

Spanish
Morocco

Spanish
Sahara

Spanish W. Africa

Stampalia
Ital. Occ.
Aegean Is.

Stellaland
So. Africa

Straits Settlements
British Colony

Japanese
Occ. WWII

Sudan
Anglo-Egyptian Govt.

Sudan
Republic

Suez Canal
Local post

Sungei Ujong, Malay State

Surinam
Dutch Colony

Postage Due
Lilac

Swaziland,　　　　Sweden　　　　　　　　　Postage Due　Local Post
Br. Protectorate

Basel　　　　　　　Geneva　　　　　　　　Zurich

Swiss Cantonals

Switzerland

Postage due　　　　　　Official　　　　War Board　　League of
　　　　　　　　　　　　　　　　　　of Trade　　　Nations

League of Nations　　　　International Labor Bureau

Switzerland

International Bureau Education

World Health Organization

United Nations, European Offices

World Meteorological Organization

Universal Postal Union
International Bureau

International Telecommunications

Franchise Stamps

SWITZERLAND

Syria, French Mandate

Syria, Kilis Prov.   Syria

Syria, Arabian Government issue, 1920

Syria, Inde-
pendence, 1920

Syria, Free French

Syrian Arab Republic

Szechwan Province, China

Tahiti
French Col.

For Ger. E. AF.

British Colony Independence
Tanganyika

Spanish Tangier

Tannou Touva

Tanzania

Van Diemensland,
now Tasmania

Tasmania
British Colony

Tete, Port. Colony

Tetuan, Spanish Colony

Thessaly, Turkish Prov.

Turkish
Stp. Ovptd.

Bulgarian Stamps Ovptd.

Greek Stamps
Ovptd.

Thrace

Thrace, Allied Occupation, 1919-1920

Thrace, Greek Occupation

Thurn & Taxis
German States

Tibet

Timor, Portuguese Colony

Timor
Newspaper

Timor
Port. Colony

Timor
War Tax 1919

Tobago
Br. Colony

Togo
Ger. Colony

Togo
Br. Occ. WWI

Togo
Fr. Occ. WWI

Togo
Fr. Colony

Togo Republic

Tolima
Col. State

Tokelau Is.
N. Z. Dep

Kingdom of Tonga, British Protectorate

Transcaucasian Federated Republics

Transjordan, See Jordan

1st Republic   **1st Br. Occupation**   **2nd Republic**

Transvaal

2nd Republic   **Pietersburg Issue, 1901**   **2nd Br. Occupation 1900-**

Lydenburg issue   **Rustenberg issue**   **Republic**   **C.S.A.R. Ovpt. Central S. African Railway**

Transvaal

Travancore Indian State   **Trengganu State, Malaya**   **Japanese Occ. WWII**

Trieste, Allied Occupation   Trieste, Jugoslav Military Govt.

Trinidad, British Colony   Trinidad and Tobago
                                    British Colony

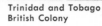

Tripoli, Ital.   Tripolitania   Tristan da Cunha   Trucial
Off. Africa   Italian Colony   Br. Colony   States, Br. Prot.
                                                             Sheikdom

Tunis, Fr. Colony   Tunis, Postage due   Tunis Republic

Turks Islands   Turks & Caicos Islands
Br. Colony   British Colony

Turkey, Ottoman Empire

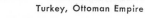

Turkey Republic

Turkey, Postage due

**Turkey,
Newspaper**

Turkey, Official

Postal Tax

Turkey in Asia (Anatolia)

**Kingdom   Provisional Govt.
Tuscany, Italian State**

**Naples
Two Sicilies**

Sicily

**Neopolitan
Provinces**

**Ubangi
French Colony**

**Uganda, Br.
Protectorate**

Uganda Republic

Ukraine (See also Western Ukraine.)

Umm Al Qiwain, Br. Protected Sheikdom

**United Arab Republic, Egypt
Occ. Palestine**

Official

United Arab Republic, Syria

United Nations

Offices in China
United States of America

Confederate States

Upper Senegal & Niger, Fr. Colony

Upper Silesia Plebescite issue

Fr. Colony
Upper Volta

Republic

Uruguay, Montevideo

Uruguay Republic

Vancouver
Island, Br.
Colony

Van
Diemensland
(Tasmania)

Vathy, Fr.
Off. Turkey

Vatican City

Vatican City

Venezia
Giulia,
Allied Mil.
Govt. WWII

Venezuela Republic

Venezuela Republic   Registration

Venezuela, Carupano Port Locals 1902-3

Venezuela,
Guayana State, 1903

Vera Cruz, Mexican
Distr. Ovpt.

Victoria, Australian State

Virgin Islands, British Colony

Wadhwan, Indian State

Wallis & Futuna Is., French Colony

Free French

Western Australia, Australian State

West Irian (West New Guinea)

Western Samoa

Укр. Н. Р.

5

Western Ukraine
Kolomea issue

Пошта
Укр.Н.Реп.

шаріз
✳   ✳
Stanislau issue

Austrian Stp. Ovptd.
Western Ukraine

Romanian Occ. 1919

White Russia
(not issued)

Wrangel Issues
For additional information and illustrations
of the issues of General Baron Peter
Wrangel, see page 135.

Wurttemberg, German State

Official   State Authorities   French Occ. WWII
                   Wurttemberg German State

Kingdom of Yemen

Kingdom of Yemen   Yemen, Postage Due

Yunnan Province, China

Yca
Chile Occ. Peru

Zambesia, Portuguese Colony

Zambia Republic

Zanzibar
British Protectorate

Zanzibar Republic

Zelaya
Nicaragua Province

Zululand
British Colony

ALPHABETS AND NUMERALS

The lure of the search, the thrill of the hunt, the satisfaction of having accomplished something different, are all part of the victory when a collector can distinguish correctly one alphabet and/or one numeral system from another.

The wide world of stamps offers many such challenges, especially in the field of the printed stamp and cancellations on stamps, covers, postcards or other postal stationery.

The following illustration shows a pair of stamps from the Japanese puppet state of Manchukuo. The center of the one stamp is printed with Chinese characters while the center of the other stamp is printed with Japanese characters.

Chinese
characters

Japanese
characters

The following illustration is that of a cover from a Turkish prisoner of war, during World War I.

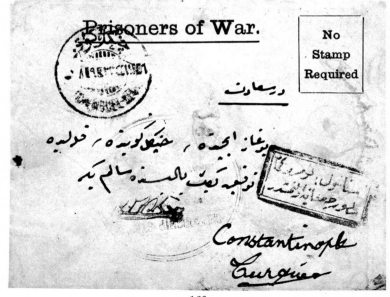

	AMHARIC (ARAB)	ARABIC ARABIA PALESTINE	ARAMAIC SYRIA, ETC.	ARMENIAN	BRAHMI (HINDU)
A	ሽ	‎ا	Υ Ϥ	Ա	ㅅ
B	∩	‎ب	ㄱ	Ր• (b,p)	◻ ▢
C	ቸ (ch)		ㅅ	Ձ‎ (ch)	ㄱ
D	ዿ	‎د ذ ض (DH)	ᐃ	Դ•(dt) Ձ(dz,+s)	Ⴓ Ⴃ
E	ዐ		ㅋ	Ե(e,y) Է֊(ēё)	Ⴑ Ⴗ
F	ፉ	‎ف	ㄱㄹ	Ֆ	♂
G	ጓ			Գ. Կ (g,k)	
H	ሀሐኀ(1,2,3)	‎ه ح	ᗺ ⊗(TH)	Հ•֊ (h',y)	ᄂ ᄔ ⊙(TH)
I			ㄱ ㄱ	Ի•	↓ ↓
J	ጀ	‎غ ج	ᔾ 2 (j,jh)		
K	ቀከኸ{k,k,kh}	‎ك خ (KH)	ㄱㄱ	ᕫ•(k,kh)	+ +
L	ለ	‎ل (MN)	ㄴ ㄴ	Լ.	ᄀ
M	መ	‎م	ㅁ ㅁ	Մ	8 Ɣ
N	ን		ㄱㄱ	Ն	⊥
O			○ ○	Ո Ո(o,oo,wo)	ㅌ
P	ጰ ፐ		ㄱㄱ	Պ(p,b) Փ(pp,ph)	ㄴ
Q		‎ق	Ϙ Ϙ		ᄒ ᄂ
R	ፈ	‎ر	ᑫ	Ռ•(r,rr)	ᄉ ᄅ
S	ሠ ስ	‎س ش ص (SH)	ㅅ Ϣ ㅂ	Ս Շ(s,sh)	ᄆ ᄆ
T	ጠጰጠ{+s,+s}	‎ت ث ط (TH)	ㄨ ㄨ	Տ(td) Ց(ts)	ㅅ ㅅ
U				Ւ	
V				Վ	
W	ወ	‎و	ㄱ Υ	Ո(wo)	◊
X					ㅈ (SH)
Y	ፕ	‎ى		Յ(y,h')	
Z	ዘዠ(z,zh)	‎ز ظ	ㅜ	Զ	ᄃ ᄐ

	CHINESE (BY SOUND)	COPTIC (EGYPT)	CYRILLIC (RUSS; SLAV & BULGAR)	DANISH (SWEDISH NORWEGIAN)	GAELIC (IRELAND)
A	挨	Ⲇ &	∂	ä	A
B	比	B ß (b,v)	В(v) Б(b)	b	b
C	絲	Ⲭ (ch, gr)	Г	c	C
D	地	Δ ∂ ⲧ ϯ ↑	Δ	d	Ꝺ
E	予	Є ε	E	e	e
F	泛	Ⴓ ч	Ф	f	Ꝼ
G	之	Ⲅ ᴦ ⲭ (soft)		g	ᵹ
H	埃	H ʜ (i, Æ)	H (L)	h	n
I	坳	I ɪ		i	ꝉ
J	坳	I ɪ	׀ (L)	ø j	
K	己	R ʀ	Ҝ	K	
L	要	Δ ∂	Λ	l	ʟ
M	吾	Ⴑ ɯ ʟ	M	m	ɯ
N	因	Ⲛ ᴨ	N	n	ɲ
O	澳	O o ~ ⲱ (long)	◊	o	O
P	彼	Ⲡ ᴨ	ᴨ	p	ꝓ
Q	丕	Ⲯ (bs)		q	
R	亞	Ⲣ ρ	◊	r	ᴦ
S	士	Ⲋ ε ~ C c	Č	s	ᴦ
T	仆	T ᴦ ~ θ (th)	T	t	ᴄ
U	左	γ	∨	u	u
V	壓	Φ (ph)		v	
W	友	Ⳓ ⲯ (sh)		w	
X	示	Ⲍ ε	Х (h)	x	
Y	為	Ⲩ ⲧ (yu)	Ү (ü)	y	
Z	於	Ⴆ (kch)	Ж(ž) Ѕ(s) З(z)	z	

	GEORGIAN	GERMAN	GREEK (ANCIENT & MODERN)	HEBREW (SEMETIC ISRAEL)	JAPANESE (BY SOUND)
A	i;	𝔄 𝔄	A	�𝓈	アイ
B	Ⴁ	𝔅	ß	﹚	ビイ
C	ჩ (ch)	ℭ	ᑦ ∧	𝆑	シイ
D	ჭ dı (d,dz)	𝔇	DΔ⊛	٦ � ᴨ	デイ
E	ᴎ	𝔈	Ϝ	٦	イー
F	Ф	𝔖	Φ F		エフ
G	Ⴓ Ⴌ (g,gh)	𝔊		ギーイ
H	Ⴈ(h') Ⴋ ჰ(hoi)	𝔖	H	ᴨ Ⴋ(TH)	エッチ
I	ᴎ	𝔍	I	'	アイ
J	ᴛ	𝔍			ジェイ
K	ᴋ ᴋᴋ ᴋʜ ᴋᴋʜ	𝔎	K	ᴑ ᴦ	ケイ
L	ᴫ	𝔏	ᴦ	�	エル
M	ᴔ	𝔐	M	ᴑ ᴑ	エム
N	Ⴉ	𝔑	∧	ᴊ ᴣ	エヌ
O	Ⴍ	𝔒 𝔒	ᴑ ◇	ᴢ	オー
P	ᴘᴜ (P,PP)	𝔓	ᴦ	ᴎ ᴨ	ピー
Q	Ⴗ	𝔔	Ϙ	ᴘ	キュー
R	ᴛ	𝔜	ᴚ	ᴦ	アール
S	ᴮ	𝔖	ᴤ	ᴥ	エス
T	ᴦᴄᴮ৪{ᵗʰ ꜰ ᵗˢʰ}	𝔗	ᴛ	ᴫ	ティー
U	Ⴍ	𝔘 𝔘	ᴠ		ユーウ
V	Ⴙ (vi)	𝔙			ヴィー
W	ᴛ (w,v)	𝔚			タブリュ
X		𝔛	X	ᴑ (sH)	エックス
Y	ᴤ	𝔜			ワイ
Z	ᴮ ᴙ (z,zh)	ᴣ	I	ᴥ	ゼット

— 163 —

	KOREAN (BY SOUND)	LATIN (ANCIENT ROME)	OLD ENGLISH	PERSIAN	RUNES (GERMANIC)
A	ㅊ (che	A	𝔄	آ ا	
B	ㅂ	B	𝔅	ب	ᛒ
C		Ↄ	ℭ	چ (ch)	ᚲ ᛣ ᚳ ᛉ
D	ㄷ	D	𝔇	د	ᚦ ᚦ ᚦ ᚦ (TH) ᛞ ᛞ H
E		Ɛ	𝔈		ᚨ ᚨ ᚩ ᚫ
F		F	𝔉	ف	ᚠ ᚹ ᛟ ᚹ
G		G	𝔊	گ - غ (gh)	ᛃ ᛜ
H	ㅎ	⊟	ℌ	ح (hʿ, h)	ᚺ ᚻ ᚺ ᚻ ᚻ
I		I	ℑ	ی	ᛁ
J	ㅈ		𝔍	ج	
K	ㄱ ㅋ	ꓘ	𝔎	ک - خ (kh)	ᚴ
L		𐌋	𝔏	ل - لا (la)	ᛚ
M	ㅁ	M	𝔐	م	ᛗ
N	ㄴ	N	𝔑	ن	ᚷ ᚾ ᚷ ᛣ
O	ㅇ	O	𝔒		ᛟ ᛟ ᛟ
P	ㅍ	𐌐	𝔓	پ	ᛈ ᛖ (e)
Q		Q	𝔔	ق (q, g)	
R	ㄹ	q	ℜ	ر	ᚱ R
S	ㅅ	𐌔	𝔖	س ص ش (sh)	ᛊ
T	ㅌ	T	𝔗	ت ط	ᛏ
U	ㅏ (AH) ㅑ (YAH) ㅓ (OH) ㅕ (YOH) ㅗ (OH) ㅛ (YO) ㅜ (OOH) ㅠ (YU) ㅡ (UH) ㅣ (EE) • (KNDR)	V	𝔘	و	ᚢ ᚢ
V			𝔙		
W			𝔚		ᚹ ᚹ
X		X	𝔛		ᚷ (g)
Y		Y	𝔜	ض (z, z)	ᛉ ᛉ ᛣ ᛦ
Z		Z	ℨ	ظ ط ژ (zh)	ᛇ ᛇ (ih, eo)

	RUSSIAN	SANSKRIT (HINDU-INDIC)	TURKISH
A	Я	म	ا
B	Б В В	ब	ب (b,f)
C	Ч (сн)	च	چ (ch)
D	Д	३ द	د (d,t)
E	E E Ь Э	ए	
F	Ф Θ		ف
G	Г	ग	چ گ (g')
H	Ж (zн) Ч (сн) Ш (sн) Щ (sнсн)	ह :	ح (k') ه
I	И Й	इ	ى (i,y)
J	К	ज	ج
K	Л	क	ك خ (kh)
L	М	ल	ل
M	Н	प ·	ر
N	О	अ ड ण	ن
O	П	भो	
P		प	پ ب (pp)
Q			ش ش (sh)
R	Р	त भ र	ر
S	С Ш (sн) Щ (sнсн)	श ह ब	
T	Т Ц (тs)	ट	ص ش
U	У	उ	ت ث (th)
V	Ю (yu)	ब	و
W			
X	Х		
Y	Ы У Ю (yu) Я (ya)	प	ى (y,i)
Z	З Ж (zн)		ظ ض ز ذ

	ARABIC (ALPHA)	ARABIC (GOBAR)	ARABIC (TURKEY)	BABY-LONIAN	BENGAL-ESE
1	١	/	١	𐎣	৸
2	ٮ	2	٢	𐎣𐎣	২
3	ٮ	?	٣	𐎣𐎣𐎣	৩
4	J	۶	٤	𐎣𐎣𐎣	8
5	٥	٤	٥	𐎣𐎣𐎣	৫
6	٩	Y	٦	𐎣𐎣𐎣	৬
7	j	✓	٧	𐎣𐎣𐎣	৭
8	ح	∧	٨	𐎣𐎣𐎣	৮
9	ط	9	٩	𐎣𐎣𐎣	৯
0	ى	/o	•	⟨	

	BURMESE	CHINESE (ROD)	CHINESE, KOREAN, JAPANESE	ANNAM., (ORDINARY) (OFFICIAL)	DANISH (SWEDISH, NORWEGIAN)
1	၁	I	一	壹	EN
2	၂	II	二	貳	TO
3	၃	III	三	叁	TRE
4	၄	IIII	四	肆	FIRE
5	၅	IIIII	五	伍	FEM
6	၆	⊤	六	陸	SE·RS
7	၇	⊤⊤	七	柒	SY·V
8	၈	⊤⊤⊤	八	捌	ATT·E
9	၉	⊤⊤⊤⊤	九	玖	NI
0	၀	—			TÉ-

	DEVAN-AGARI	EGYPTIAN (HIEROG.)	EGYPTIAN (HIERA)	GREEK (ATTIC)	GREEK (IONIAN)
1	۹	I	(	I	A
2	২	II	(I	II	B
3	३	III	(II	III	Γ
4	8	IIII	५	IIII	Δ
5	५	III II	٦	Γ	E
6	६	III III	⸌	ΓI	[F]
7	७	IIII III	₹	ΓII	Z
8	८	IIII IIII	=	ΓIII	H
9	९	IIII IIIII	?	ΓIIII	Θ
0	O	∩	⅄	△	

	HEBREW	INDIAN	KASHMIR	MALAY (PERSIAN)	MAYAN
1	א	٩	3	٠	·
2	ב	ج	3	٢	··
3	ג	३	3	٣	···
4	ד	8	I	٤	····
5	ה	५	५	٥	—
6	ו	६	٢	٦	÷
7	ז	७	‿	٧	··
8	ח	८	ॿ	٨	···
9	ט	९	৮	٩	····
0	ٮ	०	·	٠	═

	NEPALI	ROMAN	SANSKRIT	SIAMESE	CYRILLIC (RUSSIAN, SLAVONIC)
1	?	I.	?	?	Ã.
2	?	II.	?	?	Ƃ.
3	?	III.	?	?	Г̃.
4	?	IV.	?	?	Ã.
5	5	V.	?	?	Ẽ.
6	?	VI.	?	?	Ѕ̃.
7	?	VII.	?	?	З̃.
8	?	VIII.	?	?	Н̃.
9	?	IX.	?	?	Ѳ̃.
0	O	X.		O	Ї̃.

	SUMARIAN	TIBETIAN
1	▼	)
2	▼ ▼	2
3	▼▼▼	3
4		ᴝ
5		ᴧ
6		ᴠ
7	▼▼▼ ▼▼▼	ᴜ
8		ᐸ
9		ρ
0	◄	0

GLOSSARY INTRODUCTION

For many years there has been available variously condensed and abridged, abbreviated and categorized styles of a philatelic glossary. All of these printings were valuable and they did an excellent service to the collector.

The time has now come to put into better perspective the growing interest in stamp collecting generally as well as in semi-specialized philately. It is believed that the need for a broader approach to stamp collecting terminology is apparent and the more than 700 explanations of philatelic terms while by no means complete in any category, is of such interest and value as to be part of this book.

A

A—An overprint on certain stamps of South Australia indicates official correspondence of the office of the State Architect.

A—Main design of the first Registration stamps for the republic of Colombia. It stands for the Spanish word "Anotacion."

A—This double-lined watermark is the initial of the papermaker Agostino Amici. It is used on the 1 lira stamp of Modena, 1852.

A & T—These initials are found on the French colonial stamps, "Commerce" type, used in Annam and Tonkin, 1888.

ABASI—A unit of currency of Afghanistan, equals ⅓ of 1 Kabul rupee.

ACCESSORIES—When applied to stamp collecting, covers such items as hinges, tongs, perforation gauges, stock books, stock cards, stock sheets, watermark detectors, etc.

ACCOUNT LETTERS—Small letters are found printed on the bottom margin of the half-penny and one-penny British stamps in the same color as the stamps. They were used as a check on the quantity of stamps printed as well as for bookkeeping purposes. Many varieties of position exist.

ACORES—This inscription is found on the stamps of the Portuguese Colony of Azores.

A. D.—These are the initials of the engraver, M. A. Doms, as found on the stamps of Belgium, 1869-1891.

ADHESIVE—An old term indicating ordinary postage stamps which were intended to be glued or stuck on the documents, packages, letters, etc.

ADLER, C.—A man who printed the lithographed 1¼ and 2½ schilling stamps of Hamburg from 1864 to 1866.

ADMIRALTY OFFICIAL—This overprint is found on the 1902 stamps of Great Britain for use of the Admiralty Department.

ADVANCE AUSTRALIA—These words are on the standard held by the allegorical figure of Australia on the 2½ pence of New South Wales, 1891. This is also the motto of the Australian Commonwealth.

AEGEAN ISLANDS—A group of many small islands of the Aegean Sea in the Mediterranean.

AFRICA CORREIOS—This inscription means "African postage" and is found on the Vasco da Gama commemorative stamps of the Portuguese colonies in 1898.

A. G.—This overprint on certain stamps of South Australia indicates official correspondence of the Attorney-General of the state of South Australia.

AGUINALDO STAMPS—These are controversial so-called provisional stamps of the Revolutionary Government in the Philippines under Aguinaldo in 1898. They are of a local nature and were probably used only in the Revolutionary Territory controlled by Aguinaldo.

AHMNOS—This overprint is found on certain Greek stamps for use of the Greek troops during the war of 1912-13 on the islands of Lemnos.

ALBINO—A colorless impression of an embossed stamp usually found in envelope stamps.

ALBUM—With reference to stamp collecting an album is that book wherein is contained the stamp collection. An album may be in a bound book form or with a spiral binding or looseleaf post binding or in any type of ring binder. The album may have printed pages, blank pages or quadrille ruled pages.

"ALBUM WEEDS"—This is the title of one of the finest, meticulous works on forgeries in the world of stamp collecting written by the Rev. R. Brisco Earee which was last published in the year 1906.

ALESSANDRI, M.—The engraver of the dies for the first stamps of Tuscany.

ALEXANDRIE—French word for "Alexandria" used on the stamps of the French Consular Office in that city.

A. M.—This overprint was used on some of the provisional stamps of Greece of 1900. They stand for "Axia Metalliki" which means "value of coin."

AMADEUS—Spanish King, 1872-73, whose portrait appears on certain stamps of Spain.

AMERICA CENTRAL—This inscription is found on some of the stamps of El Salvador and refers to the geographical position of the republic.

AMERICAN BANK NOTE COMPANY—The title of the New York firm of engravers and printers who produced the United States stamps from 1879 to 1894.

AMHARIC—The name of the official language of Ethiopia (Abyssinia). It is of Semitic origin and has been used since the thirteenth century, written from right to left.

AMORETTI BROTHERS—The name of the firm which produced the electrotypes from which the stamps of the Roman state of Romagna were printed.

AMTLICHER VERKEHR—This inscription is found on the stamps of Wurttemberg which were for use on official communications.

ANCACHS—A department of the republic of Peru.

ANCHEL—This word means "post" and is found on the stamps of the Indian Native State of Travancore.

ANCHOR—This refers to a watermark design used by Great Britain and Cape of Good Hope. One type is known as the "fouled (or cabled) anchor" and the other one as "unfouled anchor."

ANGE-DELILE, M.—The lithographer of the stamps of Bordeaux, 1870-1871.

ANGELI, HEINRICH V.— The name of the Hungarian painter of the portrait of Queen Victoria as shown on the 2, 3 and 5 rupee stamps of India and first stamps of Southern Nigeria.

ANILINE—This is the name of color usually applied to the mauve and carmine shades. Aniline inks are soluble in water and as such were deterrents to the cleaning of canceled stamps for fraudulent purposes.

ANNA—A unit of currency usually $\frac{1}{16}$ part of a rupee and used in the Indian Native States, British East Africa, Zanzibar, British Somaliland, etc.

ANOTADO—This overprint as found on the Mexican provisional issue of 1872 indicates a reuse of an obsolete issue.

ANTILLAS PACIFICO—This inscription is found on the map stamps of Panama and refers to the Sea of Antilles.

ANTIOQUIA—A department of the republic of Colombia.

A.O.—This overprint on certain stamps of the Congo indicates Belgian occupation of German East Africa.

A.O.—This overprint on certain stamps of South Australia indicates official correspondence of the Audit Office.

A.O.F.—French West Africa.

A.O.I.—This is an overprint and inscription which means "Italian East Africa."

A.P.S.—This abbreviation stands for the American Philatelic Society of the United States.

A PAYER-TE BETALEN—This inscription is found on postage due stamps of Belgium and means "to pay." "A Payer" is French and "Te Betalen" is Flemish.

A PERCEVOIR—This inscription is found on the postage due stamps of France and colonies as well as the first postage due stamps of Belgium and means "to collect or receive."

APPROVAL BOOKS—These are booklets of stamps identified and priced by a dealer and sent out by mail to potential customers.

APURIMAC—A department of the republic of Peru.

A.R.—Several South American countries have used this inscription which means "Aviso de Recepcion" or "advice of receipt."

ARAD—In 1919 the then current Hungarian stamps were overprinted "Occupation Francaise" and appeared in Arad, a railway junction and trading center.

ARANGO, J. L.—A man who printed some of the stamps of the republic of Colombia and the Department of Antioquia.

ARCHER, HENRY—This is the name of the Irishman who first invented the machine with which to perforate postage stamps. His first machine in 1847 was unsuccessful, and in 1849 he produced another machine, and by 1854 the first regular perforated stamps were available.

ARCHER AND DALY—This is the name of the engraving and printing firm in Richmond, Virginia, who supplied the first postage stamps of the 1863 general issue for the Confederate States.

A RECEBER—This inscription is found on certain stamps of Portugal and some of the postage due stamps of the Portuguese colonies and means "to be received."

ARMENWET—This overprint is found on some stamps of the Netherlands, 1899-1910. It implied "relief of the poor."

ARMY OFFICIAL—This overprint was used on some British stamps for use within the departments of the British army, 1896.

ARMY OFFICIAL—This overprint on the 1 mill stamp of Sudan was for official army correspondence.

ARMY SERVICE—This overprint is found on the stamps of Sudan, 1906-08, and was used for official correspondence of the army.

ARTIGAS—This name along with a new date and value was surcharged on some of the stamps of Uruguay in 1911 in memory of General Artigas, the father of the Uruguan Republic.

ARVIZKAROSULTAKNAK KULON— This inscription which reads "for the flood sufferers, extra" is found in the label below the design of the stamp of Hungary, 1913.

A.S.D.A.—These initials stand for the American Stamp Dealers' Association.

ASSISTENCIA—This overprint means "to assist" or "to aid" and is found on some of the stamps of Portugal and the Azore Islands of 1912 and 1913.

A.T.—This abbreviation, meaning "Army Telegraph," was overprinted on some of the stamps of the Orange Free State along with letters "V.R.I." and were used during the Boer War by the British army in the Orange River Colony.

AT BETALE—This inscription, meaning "to pay," is found on the postage due stamps of Norway.

ATHENS PRINTS—This title refers to the stamps of Greece printed in Athens in 1861-99.

ATT—A unit of currency of Siam which was $\frac{1}{64}$ part of 1 tical.

AUCKLAND EXHIBITION—This overprint is found on stamps of New Zealand commemorating the Exhibition at Auckland in 1913.

AUNUS—Finnish spelling for the Russian town of Olonets which was captured by the Finnish troops in 1919. Stamps of Finland overprinted "Aunus" were put in use for the limited time that the town remained under Finnish military control.

AUR—A unit of value of Iceland. The aur was $\frac{1}{100}$ part of a krona.

AUSTRIAN CRETE—Stamps of Austrian design with values surcharged "centimes" or "franc" instead of heller and kronen.

AUSTRIAN ITALY—Designs of Austrian stamps with the values expressed in centesimi or "centes." The currency was later changed to soldi.

AUSTRIAN LEVANT—Stamps of Austrian design with values in "soldi." The values were later changed to "para" and "piaster."

AVISO DE RECEPCION—This inscription is found on the Acknowledgment of Receipt stamps of El Salvador.

AVISPORTO-MAERKE—This inscription is found on the stamps of Denmark for the prepayment of postage on newspapers sent to non-subscribers.

AVO—A unit of value of Macao and Timor valued at about $\frac{1}{100}$ of 1 pataca.

AYACUCHO—A department of the republic of Peru.

AYTONOMOE—This word is found on some stamps of Albania and Epirus, a Greek word which means "autonomous."

B

B—When found on the various stamps of the Straits Settlements, indicates use at Bangkok, British Office.

B—The letter "B" is found under the bust of French stamps of 1862 as the initial of the engraver, M. Barre.

B—Is sometimes found overprinted with "Depto. Zelaya" when on stamps of Nicaragua in the wealthy Bluefields area.

B.A.—This overprint means "British Administration Government" of Eritrea and Somaliland in 1950.

BADEN-POWELL—Major-General Sir Robert Baden-Powell is also known as the hero of the Siege of Mafeking during the Boer War, 1899-1900. His portrait appeared on the local stamps used within Mafeking only. He was also the founder of the International Boy Scout movement.

BAJOCCHO—A unit of value of the Roman states, equivalent to $\frac{1}{100}$ of a scudo.

BALBOA—A unit of value in the republic of Panama. 1 balboa is equal to 100 centimos. The name of this currency is derived from that of Vasco Nunez de Balboa, Spanish explorer and discoverer of the western seas in 1501 and the Pacific Ocean in 1513. Balboa was executed in 1517 by jealous enemies.

BALLON MONTE OR BALLOON POST —The famous Balloon Post of the Franco-Prussian War of 1870-71 was the only method of communication from the city of Paris to the outside world. While the city was surrounded by German troops, there were some sixty-five individual balloons used during this time, all of which had an individual name. Some of the names were Le Neptune, Le Celeste, Le George Sand, Le Washington, Le Victor Hugo, Le Montgolfier, Le Gallilee, Le Jacquard, Le Franklin, Le General Renault, La Gironde, La Ville de Florence, La Poste de Paris, General Cambronne, General Bourbaki, General Faidherbe, etc. Much of this balloon mail reached its destination, although a few balloons were destroyed by the Germans and through causes attributed to winds. All letters carried on the balloons were usually marked "Par Ballon Monté."

BALCOCA, R.—This is the name of the artist who painted "Columbus Announcing His Discovery" which design was used for the 15 cent stamp of the United States Columbian issue of 1893.

BAN—The plural of ban is bani and is a unit of value in Romania. 1 ban is equal to $\frac{1}{100}$ of 1 leu.

BANAT-BACSKA—This was a district of old Hungary divided between Jugoslavia and Romania in 1919 during the Romanian occupation. Certain stamps of Hungary were overprinted.

BANCO Y CASA DE MONEDA—The printing establishment which produced the stamps of Buenos Aires in Argentina.

BARANYA—During the Serbian occupation of Hungary in 1919, stamps of Hungary were overprinted "Baranya" in both the *first* and *second* occupation.

BARCLAY & FRY—The printing establishment at which the stamps of Shanghai issue of 1893 were engraved and printed.

BARNARD, J.—This man lived in Port Louis on the island of Mauritius and is famous for having engraved the dies of the world famous "Post Office" stamps of Mauritius issued in 1847. He was a watchmaker and jeweler and the only man on the island who could engrave a die. It is said that Lady Gomm, the wife of the then British Governor of the island, being anxious to use the new fad of postage stamps on her invitations to her fancy dress ball to be held at the governor's mansion, put such pressure on Mr. Barnard that he used the words "post office" instead of "postpaid." After this error was discovered, Mr. Barnard also engraved the new plates "post paid" instead of "post office" in 1848. The "post office" Mauritius one-penny orange and two-penny blue are worth today in excess of $25,000 for each stamp.

BARTH-WAHL, M.—The engraver of the plates of the first stamps of Luxemburg.

BASTED MILLS—The name of the paper manufacturing company in Kent, England, who supplied the thin-hard paper watermarked with a double lined "N Z" and a star for some of the half-penny and one-penny stamps of New Zealand, 1901.

BATONNE PAPER—This paper has a watermark of straight parallel lines which it acquires during manufacture. It has been used in the production of stamps of many countries. It is usually divided into two categories:

"Laid Batonne": While this type of paper is seldom seen, it is interesting to note that the spaces between the watermark lines seem to have lighter additional watermark lines running parallel. Some stamps from the Mexican state of Guadalajara have been printed on this type of paper.

"Wove Batonne": In this type of watermark, lines are clear without any lines between them. Some Indian Native states have made use of this type.

BAYER, POSTTAXE—This inscription is found on the first postage due stamps of Bavaria, meaning "Bavarian Postal Tax."

B.C.A.—This overprint is found on the stamps of the British South Africa Company for use in Northern Rhodesia and Nyasaland, as British Central Africa.

B.C.M.—These initials mean "British Consular Mail" used in Madagascar.

B.C.O.F.—These initials mean "British Commonwealth Occupational Force." On May 8, 1847, through February 12, 1949, stamps of Australia, etc., were thus overprinted for use of the British troops in the occupation of Japan.

B. C.—This overprint is found on some stamps of South Australia and was for official use of the Barracks Department.

BELGIE POSTERIJEN—This inscription is found on Belgium stamps of 1891-96 and means "Belgium Post" in Flemish.

BENGASI—This North African seaport in Tripoli was the seat of the Italian Consular office using stamps of Italy overprinted "Bengasi" and the value in piastres.

BESA—A unit of value in the Italian Consular area of Benadir in Italian Somaliland. 1 besa was equivalent to ¼ of 1 anna.

BEST, H. & C.—The name of printers of the first stamps of Tasmania, then known as Van Diemen's Land.

BEY, NAZIM—This is the name of the Turkish artist who designed the stamps of Turkey for the 1908 issue showing the Tughra of Sultan Mohammed V.

B. G.—This overprint is found on some stamps of South Australia and indicates official use by the Botanical Garden Department.

B. G.—These letters were found on the newspaper stamps of Modena in 1853 and mean "Bollo Gazzette" or "Stamp for Journal."

B. HIIEIPOE—This surcharge is found on the 1913 Greek occupation issue for use in Northern Epirus.

BI-COLORED—This refers to stamps printed in two different colors.

BISECT—A bisect usually refers to a provisional or emergency issue of stamps. They were usually cut in half or in half on an angle, thereby reducing the face value by one-half. In some cases the bisect was done by perforating the stamp and surcharging each perforated half with the new value. Bisects are known from Haiti and many British colonies, etc.

B.I.T.—These initials mean "Bureau Internationale du Travail" or "International Labour Office" on stamps of Switzerland.

BIT—A unit of value in the former Danish West Indies (now U. S. Virgin Islands) equivalent to ¹⁄₁₀₀ of 1 franc.

BIT—This is the name of the small, usually metallic devices attached to the dandyroll for impressing watermarks during the manufacture of paper.

B. L. C. I.—These letters are found in the four corners of the design on several stamps of the Indian state of Bhopal. The "B.L." stands for "Bhopal" and "C.I." stands for "Central India."

BLOCK OF FOUR—This term refers to four stamps in an unsevered block of two stamps in two rows of two each.

BLOOD, D. O. & CO.—A private post company in the United States, established in Philadelphia in 1843 for the delivery of local letters.

BLUE PAPER—The United States issued certain stamps in 1908-09 printed on a paper of a high rag content as an experiment. The finished product looked bluish gray on the front as well as on the back of the stamps. This is not to be confused with the Blue Safety Paper.

BLUE SAFETY PAPER—This was a paper by De La Rue & Company in the manufacture of certain stamps of Great Britain in 1855. In order to prevent fraudulent reuse of these stamps by the cleaning of the cancellations, a certain amount of prussiate of potash salt was added in the process of paper manufacture which when combined with minute particles of iron in the paper pulp brought about a bluish look.

BLUED PAPER—This is usually referred to when speaking of the early line engraved printing stamp by Perkins, Bacon & Co. for Great Britain and colonies. The bluing was caused by one or more ingredients of the printing ink running into the paper.

B. M.—This overprint is found on some stamps of South Australia and was for the official use of the Board of Magistrates.

B.M.A.—These initials mean "British Military Administration" on stamps of Sarawak, Malaya, etc.

B.N.F.—These initials are found on certain stamps of Castellorizo during the French occupation, 1920, and mean "Base Navale Francaise."

BOARD OF EDUCATION—This overprint is found on certain stamps of Great Britain and was for official correspondence from the Board of Education.

BOLIVAR—A department of the republic of Colombia.

BOLIVAR—A province of the republic of Ecuador.

BOLIVAR—A unit of value in the republic of Venezuela. 100 centimos equals 1 bolivar.

BOLIVAR, SIMON—This man is often referred to as the "Liberator" of South America from the Spanish rule. He is also known as the father of the republic of Venezuela, etc. His portrait is found on many stamps from the various countries of South America.

BOLIVIANO—A unit of value in the republic of Bolivia. 100 centavos equals 1 boliviano.

BOLLO DELLA POSTA NAPOLETANA—This inscription is found on the stamps of Naples and means "Stamp of the Neapolitan Post."

BOLLO POSTALE—This inscription is found on the stamps of San Marino and means "postage stamp."

BOND PAPER—This is a fine grade of strong paper made from linen rags and upon which several die proofs of United States stamps may be found.

BORDEAUX PRINTS—During the Siege of Paris in 1870-1871, French stamps were lithographed at Bordeaux due to the inability of the Paris Mint to supply.

BOYACA—A department of the republic of Colombia.

B. R. A.—These initials stand for "British Railway Administration" and are found overprinted on the half-cent stamp of China, 1898. The stamps were in use for about one month.

BRADBURY, WILKINSON & COMPANY—The name of a famous firm of printers and engravers in London, England. Some of the stamps printed by this firm were nineteenth century issues for the Falkland Islands, British South Africa Company, British East Africa Company, etc.

BRAUNSCHWEIG—This is the German spelling for the state of Brunswick of the German Empire.

BRITISH AMERICAN BANK NOTE COMPANY—The printing firm from which emanate practically all of the stamps of Canada since 1868. It is also known as the Canadian Branch of the American Bank Note Company.

BRITISH CONSULAR MAIL—In order to prepay mail to Port Louis, Mauritius or the Reunion Islands, the then British Vice Council at Madagascar authorized the issue of very large stamps. The service lasted about three years.

BRITISH INLAND MAIL—This was a local mail service between Antananarivo and Vatomandry on the island of Madagascar. This service only lasted a few months.

BRITISH LEVANT—The British government maintained Consular Post Offices in the then Ottoman Empire of Turkey and in 1905 current British stamps were overprinted "Levant" for use by these offices.

BRITISH SOUTH AFRICA COMPANY—This inscription is found on stamps of Rhodesia prior to 1906. Through the efforts of Sir Cecil Rhodes, the British South Africa Company was formed in Rhodesia to promote trade and commerce and to develop the natural resources of that area.

BROZIK, W.—This is the name of the painter of the famous "Columbus Soliciting Aid of Isabella" which was reproduced on the 5-cent Columbian Commemorative stamp of 1893.

BRUXELLES—This is the French spelling of Brussels and is shown on the Belgian Commemorative stamps of 1896.

BUITEN BEZIT—This overprint is found on the stamps of the Dutch East Indies of 1908. It was used to determine the volume of mail within the Dutch East Indies with the exception of Java and Madura.

BULL'S EYES—This name is applied to the 1843 issues of Brazilian stamps. They were so named because of their design.

BURELAGE—This philatelic term is usually applied to a covering of the stamp with a group of fine lines or dots. These may be straight lines or wavy lines. Stamps of Denmark and Danzig have good examples of burelage.

BUSHIRE—The name of the Persian port in the Persian Gulf occupied by British troops during World War I. Stamps from the 1911-1915 issue of Persia were overprinted "BUSHIRE—UNDER BRITISH OCCUPATION." The stamps were in use for only a few months.

C

C—This overprint is found on some stamps of South Australia and is for the official use of the Customs Department.

C. A.—These letters are sometimes found on stamps of Nicaragua indicating the geographical position of the Nicaraguan Republic in Central America.

CABO—An overprint of some of the stamps of Nicaragua which started about 1904. The word "Cabo" refers to "Cabo Gracias a Dios," a seaport and cape in northeastern Nicaragua.

CABOT, JEAN—The discoverer of Newfoundland who is featured on the set of commemorative stamps of Newfoundland in 1897.

CABO VERDE—This inscription is found on the stamps of the Portuguese colony of Cape Verde Islands.

CAISSE D'AMORTISSEMENT—This is the French expression for a "sinking fund" and is found on semi-postal stamps of France in 1928-30 etc.

CALIMNO—This overprint is found on the stamps of Italy for use in the Calimno Island in the Aegean Sea.

CAMEROONS, U.K.T.T.—This overprint on certain stamps of Nigeria means "United Kingdom Trust Territory."

CANAL MARITIME DE SUEZ—This is the inscription used on the private stamps of the Suez Canal Company, 1868.

CANARIAS—This is the Spanish name for the Canary Islands off the northwest coast of Africa in the Atlantic Ocean.

CANCELLATION—A mark of obliteration or cancelling of the stamp to show that it is no longer valid for postal duty. This can be done by marking devices or pens or cuts, etc.

CANCELLED-TO-ORDER—In the past many countries sold remainders of stocks of stamps at a discount from face value by applying a specific type of bar cancellation. Today the same thing is being done with the exception that the stamp is nicely and neatly cancelled to make it a collector's item.

CANDAREEN—A unit of value as shown on the early stamps of Shanghai. 1 candareen was $1/100$ of a tael.

CANDARIN—A unit of value of the stamps of China up to 1897. A candarin was $1/100$ of a tael.

CANTONAL STAMPS—These are stamps issued by and for use in the Swiss cantons of Zurich and Geneva and the city of Basle; from Basle was issued the very popular stamp showing a dove.

CAP OF LIBERTY—This symbol is found in the postage stamps of Haiti, Paraguay, Salvador, etc., and as the watermark on certain "Seebeck" issues of Ecuador, Nicaragua and Salvador.

CAPPED NUMERALS—The 2¢ value of the United States 1890 issue is the stamp usually referred to as with the variety of capped numerals, either on the right numeral or the left numeral; these caps were caused by defective transfer rolls.

CARLIST STAMPS—These stamps were issued in Spain by the Carlists during the insurrection of 1873-1874.

CARITAS—This inscription is found on various charity stamp issues of Belgium and Luxemburg.

CAROL I, REGE AL ROMANIEI—This inscription means "Charles I, King of the Romanians" and is shown on the 1903 issue of Romania's stamps.

CARRIERS' STAMPS—These were stamps of the United States which were used during 1861 to defray the postage from a post office to the addressee residing in the same postal district.

CARTER'S PAID DESPATCH—This was a Philadelphia local post established in 1849.

CARTOPHILY—This was the name formerly used to identify collecting of postal cards.

CARTRIDGE PAPER—This is a paper usually with a rough surface and used to print some of the one-penny stamps of Trinidad, 1853.

CASH—This was a unit of value in Shanghai, 10 cash were equal to 1 candarin.

CATALOG—All stamp collectors use a standard stamp catalog which lists and identifies through proper classification postage stamps of the world.

CATHARINE WHEEL—This phrase is seldom heard anymore, but it refers to the wheeled overprint on many stamps of the republic of Salvador in 1899 and 1900 to distinguish stamps as actually used compared to the un-overprinted remainders in the hands of contractors.

CAVE—This overprint is found across the face of many stamps of Ceylon. It was the name of a business firm in Ceylon and was used to prevent pilfering of postage stamps by employees.

C.CH.—This overprint is sometimes found on the "Commerce" design stamps of France which were used in Cochin, China, during 1886.

C.D.—This overprint is found on certain stamps of South Australia during 1868-1874 which were used for official correspondence of the Convict Department.

C.E.F.—This overprint is found on many stamps of India and means "China Expeditionary Force." The stamps were used mainly by British forces in China during the Boxer Rebellion.

C.E.F.—When applied as an overprint to German colonial stamps, these initials mean "Cameroons Expeditionary Force." The stamps were used by the British forces occupying this German colony in 1915.

CENT—A unit of value of many countries and represents $1/100$ part of a dollar.

CENTAVO—A unit of value of most South and Central American countries. A centavo is usually $1/100$ of a peso.

CENT DE ESCUDO—This denomination is sometimes seen on the stamps of Spain and colonies. One cent de escudo was usually $1/100$ of 1 escudo.

CENT DE PESETA—This unit of value is found on stamps of Spain and colonies. 1 cent was about $1/100$ of a peseta.

CENTENNIAL—The name of a 100th anniversary of an important event such as birthdays, deaths or treaties, etc.

CENTERED—This very controversial term is used when it is meant that the four framed lines of the stamp are perfectly centered within the perforation or within the borders of the stamp paper.

CENTES.—This is short for "centesimi" which was a unit of value during 1850-1858 in Austrian Italy. 100 centesimi were equal to 1 lira.

CENTESIMO—A unit of value which appears on the stamps of Italy and Uruguay. 100 centesimos were equal to 1 lira in Italy and 100 centesimos were equal to 1 peso in Uruguay.

CENTIME—A unit of value found on many stamps of France and colonies, Belgium, etc. 100 centimes were equal to 1 franc.

CENTIMETRE—As a unit of metric measurement, it is mostly used on the philatelic perforation gauges, such as the unique new "WHIT-PERF" gauge, to measure the perforations on practically all stamps of the world. Two centimetres is equal to 20 millimeters.

CENTIMO—A unit of value which is found on the stamps of Spain, Costa Rica, Dominican Republic, etc. 1 centimo is $1/100$ of a peso or peseta, etc.

CENTER LINE—This is where the horizontal and vertical guide lines cross on a sheet of stamps.

CERES DESIGN—The symbolic design of Liberty as applied to France was the head of Ceres as shown on the stamps of 1849-1850, 1870-1875, 1945-1947, etc.

CERTIFICADO—This inscription is found on stamps for registration of mail from certain Spanish speaking countries.

C. F. A.—This overprint is found on stamps of France for use in Reunion Island and means "Colonies Francaise d'Afrique."

CHAHI—A unit of value in the old Persian monetary system. A chahi was equivalent to $1/20$ of 1 kran.

C.G.H.S.—These initials were overprinted on Prussian and German official stamps for use in Upper Silesia.

— 177 —

CHAKRA—This name is applied to the watermark of the Siamese stamps of 1887. (Whitman No. 291.)

CHALK SURFACED PAPER—A paper used in the manufacture of certain postage stamps which was coated with a mixture usually containing artificial barium sulphate. This gave the surface a chalky appearance and prevented cleaning of cancellations from the stamp for re-use. This type of paper was used for several years in the printing of stamps for various British colonies.

CHALON, ALFRED EDWARD, R. A.—Was born in Geneva, Switzerland. In 1837 he painted the gracious full-length portrait of the young, attractive Queen Victoria. Many of the most beautiful classic stamps of the British Empire were designed from the famous Chalon portrait.

CHAMBERS' PERFORATION—This was a private perforation used in 1911 by the J. V. Farwell Company of Chicago, wholesale dry goods merchants. It consisted of eight holes for each side which were arranged in two groups of four each.

CHARITY STAMPS—These stamps have been issued by many countries and more often than not are referred to as semipostal stamps. The surtax or additional value over the postage rate shown on the stamps was given to certain deserving or designated charities.

CHEMINS DE FER SPOORWEGEN—This inscription is found on the Belgian parcel post and railway .postage stamps, reading in French and Flemish.

CHEUN—A unit of value found on the earlier stamps of the kingdom of Korea. 1 cheun was equal to 5 poon.

CHIFFRE TAXE—This inscription is found on many postage stamps of France and certain French colonies. The literal translation is "Figure Tax," which means the amount of postage due as indicated in the large figure of the design.

CHINE—This is the French spelling for China and is found on the stamps issued for use of French offices in China.

CHINESE TREATY PORTS—During the time when foreign powers maintained a mail service through their consular offices in China, there were certain ports which were considered open ports for business, etc., and from which these consular offices dispatched mail. The British mail could use Hong Kong stamps, the French mail could use French stamps overprinted China, etc.

"CHOPS"—A first rate example of the Japanese chop, also known as ideograph, is found on the stamps of the Dutch East Indies and British Malaya, etc., as hand stamped or overprinted during the Japanese occupation of these territories during World War II.

CHOSEN—This is the Japanese spelling for the country of Korea.

CHUCKRAM—A unit of value found on the stamps of the Indian Native State of Travancore. 2 chuckrams were equal to 1 anna.

C. I. S.—This overprint means "Commission Interallie Slesvig" and is found on Schleswig official stamps.

CITY DISPATCH POST—This was a local post service established in New York in 1842.

CITY EXPRESS POST—This was a local post established in Philadelphia in 1848.

C. L.—This overprint is found on some stamps of South Australia and which were for official use of the Department of Crown Lands.

CLARKE'S CIRCULAR EXPRESS—This was a local post established in New York in 1863.

CLARK & CO.—A local post in New York City in 1857.

CLASSIC STAMPS—This term does not necessarily mean an old stamp as much as it does refer to a true philatelic item—classic in either its design, such as the first issues of most all of the older nations, or classic in itself because of being almost unique, such as the inverted center of the 1918 United States airmail.

CLEANED STAMPS—Stamps which have been put through a cleaning process to remove the cancellation so that they could be fraudulently re-used for their face value.

COIL STAMPS—Stamps sold in coil rolls, perforated either vertically or horizontally, primarily for use in stamp vending machines. Coil stamps are usually collected in pairs as well as singles.

COLIS POSTEAUX—An overprint on the French colonial stamps which indicates that they are for use on packages and parcels.

COLON—This is the Spanish form for the word Columbus and is often found on the stamps of Spanish speaking countries.

COLON—This is a unit of currency of Costa Rica since 1901. 100 centavos equals 1 colon.

COLONES—This is the plural of the word "colon," currency of Costa Rica.

COLONIA DE RIO DE ORO—This inscription is found on the stamps of the Spanish colony of Rio de Oro and means "Colony of Gold River."

COLONIAL PRINTINGS—This expression is used especially in reference to stamps printed in the various British colonies from impressions of the plates supplied by London.

COLLECTOR'S CLUB OF NEW YORK—The leading philatelic club in the United States formed to stimulate interest in philately and philatelic reference work. One of the finest libraries of philatelic references is on the premises of the club in New York City.

COLOR—This specifically refers to the tint or shade of color in which a given stamp is printed and issued. It is, however, one of the most controversial subjects in all of stamp collecting. Very seldom do any two people agree on the NAME of any shade or tint of color.

COLOR CHANGES—Many changes in color or occur accidentally over a period of time due to various forms of natural oxidation. For example, a bright orange color can change to a rusty-brown. Pigments used in preparing the ink for many stamps issued during the nineteenth century were not mixed with the precision of today. The result is that we may have ten distinctly different shades of a given color. Other changes are deliberately made with the intent to defraud. The use of a standardized philatelic color reference is the best insurance of identifying a specific color.

COLOR TRIALS—In the past, selected designs for new stamps were printed in various colors as a trial prior to being presented to the Post Office Department and to committees in charge of selecting colors. Few of these color trial impressions become available to the stamp collector but are found in museums where philatelic history is maintained.

COMB PERFORATIONS—Stamps which have been perforated by comb machine are regular perforated on three sides at one time, the machine moves the sheet up to perforate the next row, etc.

COMMEMORATIVE STAMPS—Stamps that are issued in commemoration of a great event in the history of the originating nation or some great event in world history. The United States presently issues approximately fifteen commemorative stamps each year. Certain other countries have issued from ten to twenty commemorative stamps each month.

COMPANHIA DE MOCAMBIQUE—This inscription is found on the stamps issued by the Portuguese Mozambique Company.

COMPOUND PERFORATION—A stamp which has two different perforation measurements along the top and bottom, and the sides.

CONCH SHELL—This is a watermark design which is found on the stamps of Travancore, an Indian Native State.

CONDOMINIUM—This is an overprint which is found on certain stamps of New Caledonia which were previously overprinted "Nouvelles-Hebrides." The condominium overprint marked the establishment of a dual French and British government in the New Hebrides Islands.

CONFEDERATE STATES STAMPS—The title refers to the stamps issued by the Confederate States of America during the Civil War. There are many rare and expensive postmaster and area provisionals as well as those known as the general issues.

CONNELL—The Honorable Charles Connell was the Postmaster-General of New Brunswick whose controversial decision to use his own portrait on the New Brunswick 5¢ stamp of 1860 without authority created one of the most interesting stories of the philatelic world.

CONSULAR POST OFFICES—Prior to World War I many of the great nations of the world maintained post offices in the Turkish Empire, China, etc. Usually the stamps of the country represented by the Consular Post Office were overprinted with the name of the country within which they were to be used.

CONTINENTAL BANK NOTE ISSUES—In 1873 the Continental Bank Note Company used the same designs for the U. S. stamps as those of the 1870-71 issue, as printed by the American Bank Note Company, except they added certain minute identification marks, familiarly known as "secret marks."

CONTROL NUMBERS—While there are many types of control numbers that are found on the large borders or selvage of the sheets of printed stamps, one of the most obvious types of control numbers is found on the back of the stamps of Spain, during the reign of King Alfonso XIII.

CORDOBA—This is a unit of currency in the republic of Nicaragua, 1914. 100 centavos equals 1 cordoba.

COREE—This is the French spelling of Korea, and is found on the stamps of 1902 and 1903 which were printed in Paris.

CORREOS—This inscription is found on many stamps of different Spanish speaking countries and means "postage."

CORRIENTES—A province of the republic of Argentina.

COUNTERFEITS—Refers to stamps made to defraud governments as well as collectors. There have been many articles and books written about counterfeiters such as Sperati, Fournier, DeThuin, etc.

COWAN PAPER—This refers to the paper upon which the postage stamps of New Zealand were printed starting in 1902 and has a single lined N.Z. and star watermark, manufactured by Cowan and Son Ltd. in London.

C. P.—An overprint found on certain stamps of South Australia which were used for the official correspondence of the Department of the Commissioner of Police, 1868-1874.

C. POSTE—The stamps of Sardinia and the first stamps of the kingdom of Italy had this inscription. The letter "C" refers to "centesimi" and the face value of the stamp.

COVER—An entire envelope with stamps and/or cancellation, commemorative or regular issue.

C. R.—These initials are found on the stamps of the Fiji Islands, 1871. They stand for the name of King Cakobau who was deposed in 1874.

CRACKED PLATE—When stamps have been printed from plates which have cracked there will be a noticeable though usually irregular line for the extent of the crack, through the design of the stamp. Plates would crack if they were improperly hardened or if some accident had occurred.

CRAZIA—This is a unit of value used in the former Grand Duchy of Tuscany. 12 crazia were equal to 1 lira.

CREASE—When a stamp has been creased by folding or careless handling, the stamp has been damaged insofar as its value is concerned.

CROWN—There were many different types of crowns used as watermark designs in various countries in the world, such as Great Britain, Hungary, Italy, Denmark, etc., each national design being representative of its country. See Whitman watermark book for more reference.

CROWN A—This watermark design is found in the later issues of the states within the Commonwealth of Australia as well as the early issues of the Australian Commonwealth. It consists of a crown above a large letter "A" representing Australia.

CROWN C A—This watermark design shows the crown over the letters "C A" representing Crown Agents and was in use in many British colonies starting about 1882. There are three varieties of this watermark.

CROWN C C—This is another watermark showing the crown over the letters "C C" representing Crown Colonies. There are two varieties of this watermark.

CROWN E. T.—This is a watermark in the stamps of Greece which started in 1901 and means "Ellenikon Tachydromeion" or "Greek postage."

CROWN GvR—This is a watermark used in the stamps of Great Britain since 1912 up to about 1935 and is a crown over script capital letters.

CROWN N S W—This is a watermark design with a crown over the letters "N S W" and was for use in the Austrian state of New South Wales between 1871 and 1905.

CROWN Q—This is a watermark used in the Australian state of Queensland from 1868-1906.

CROWN S A—This is a watermark used in the Australian state of South Australia and consisted of a crown over the letters "S A."

CROWN V—This is a watermark used in the Australian state of Victoria which consists of a crown over the letter "V."

CROWN W A—This is a watermark used in the Australian state of Western Australia and consists of a crown over the letters "W A."

C. S.—This is an overprint found on certain stamps of South Australia between 1868-1874; they were for the official use of the Chief Secretary.

C.S.A.—This watermark appears in the paper ordered by the Confederate States of America from England.

C. SGN.—This overprint is found on some early stamps of South Australia between 1868-1874; they were for the official use of the Colonial Surgeon.

C. T.—This overprint is found on some early stamps of South Australia prior to 1874 and were for the official use of the Commissioner of Titles.

CUARTO—A unit of value of currency in old Spain. 1 cuarto is equal to ⅛ of 1 real.

CUMMING'S CITY POST—This was a local post of New York City during 1846.

CURRENCY STAMPS—This term should not be confused with "Encased Postage" currency. Currency stamps were actually issued by the imperial government of Russia in 1915-1917, and were printed on a thin type of cardboard. The inscription on the back reads: "Having circulation on a par with silver subsidiary

coins." Various denominations of stamps were so printed.

CUT SQUARES—The squared cutting of embossed envelope stamps from the envelope, leaving a substantial border around the stamp.

CUTTING'S DESPATCH POST—This was a local post in Buffalo, New York, during 1848.

CUT-TO-SHAPE—This term is used when a stamp has been trimmed to the outline of its design and particularly refers to postage stamps of early India which were octagonal in design and were usually trimmed to the borders of the design before being used. It also refers to the close trimming of embossed envelopes.

D

D—Certain stamps of the Dutch East Indies were overprinted with an uncolored "D" contained within a circle of solid color which stood for the Dutch word "Dienst" meaning "Service."

DAI NIPPON 2602—This inscription means "Empire of Japan." During World War II the Japanese army and navy occupied areas in the Pacific and Southeast Asia and overprinted the stamps of the occupied countries with inscriptions in English as well as chop marks of Japanese native characters in Katakana or Kanji script.

Malaya: Certain stamps of Straits Settlements were overprinted by Japanese military authorities during World War II for use in Negri Sembilan, Pahang, Perak, Selangor, and Trengganu during the occupation.

Yubin: Certain stamps of Perak and Selangor were overprinted to signify Japanese occupation during World War II.

DAMUS PETEMUS QUE VICISSIM—This inscription is found on certain stamps of British Guiana and means "We give and we seek in turn."

DANDY-ROLL—The dandy-roll determines whether the paper pulp passing under becomes wove, quadrille, laid, etc., type. It is also the dandy-roll that applies the pressure for the watermark designs.

DANUBE STEAM NAVIGATION COMPANY—This was a private post which operated between certain cities of Bulgaria, Romania and Serbia along the Danube River and Black Sea. Having been authorized as a private post by the Austro-Hungarian government, the service also extended into Austria and Hungary. The service commenced in 1865 and ended about 1874.

DATIA—This is the spelling of the Native Indian State of Duttia as shown on their stamps of 1897.

DAWK—Hindu word for "post."

D. B.—This overprint is found on certain stamps of the Australian state of South Australia and indicates official use by the Destitute Board.

"DEATH MASK" DESIGN—This expression refers to the lower values of the stamps of the kingdom of Serbia issued in 1904. If this stamp design is placed upside down, a third face is distinctly visible. While this is a freak of engraving, rumors had it that the third face was a reproduction of the death mask of the murdered King Alexander.

DEFICIENTE—This inscription means "deficient" and is found on the stamps of Ecuador and Nicaragua for postage due.

DEFICIT—Found on the stamps of Peru, meaning the same as postage due.

DE LA RUE & CO.—This is the name of a well known firm of engravers and printers of London. This firm printed the majority of the stamps for the British colonies and Great Britain up to about 1911.

DEMONETIZED—Stamps that have become obsolete and declared no longer valid for postage.

DENOMINATION—The face value of the stamp in the currency of the country of issue, either as the original value or in a surcharged (thereby changed) face value. (See Surcharge.)

DEPARTMENTAL STAMPS—These are usually known as official stamps and have a specific design or overprint for the use of a designated governmental department.

DIADEM—This refers to the symbol of royalty such as a crown or tiara shown on the heads of Kings and Queens on postage stamps.

DICKENSON PAPER—This is a paper invented by one' John Dickenson back in 1839. This paper has silk threads in its composition in order to prevent counterfeiting or washing of cancellations for fraudulent re-use. Certain early stamps of Switzerland, Great Britain and Bavaria provide good examples of types of silk paper.

DIE—This usually refers to the original engraved metal form from which plates are made for the actual printing of stamps.

DIE PROOF—An impression of the stamp design, usually on fine heavy white paper or bristol, from a die engraved or prepared for evaluation and submitted for selection.

DINAR—This was a unit of value of Serbia before World War I. This unit is also in use today in Jugoslavia; the Jordan dinar became effective in 1951. There are 100 paras in 1 dinar.

DINERO—This was a unit of value and is shown upon the early stamps of Peru.

DOCKWRA—It was in London in 1680 that William Dockwra originated a postal service using postmarks to indicate the place of posting, date and time. Since the year 1680 the evolution of postmarks has come to the type used today.

DOUBLE IMPRESSION—This happens when a stamp is printed twice on the face and both impressions are visible. These varieties are reasonably scarce and are much sought after by collectors.

DOUBLE LINED LETTERS—Usually refers to the watermark where the letters or numerals are in double lined design, etc.

DOUGLAS CITY DISPATCH—This was a local post in the city of New York established in 1879.

D. P.—This overprint is found on some stamps of Hong Kong and are a type of pre-cancellation indicating "Daily Press." They were applied to prevent pilfering by employees.

D. R.—This overprint is found on some stamps of the Australian state of South Australia and indicates official use of the Department of Deeds and Registration.

DRACHMA—This is a unit of currency in Greece and was also used in Crete, etc. There are 100 lepta in 1 drachma.

DRZAVA S.H.S.—Overprinted on imperial stamps of Bosnia of 1906-17 for use in Bosnia-Herzegovina as part of the new Jugoslavia Kingdom in 1918.

DUPUY & SCHENK—This was a private penny post in New York City during 1846.

E

E—This is an overprint found on some stamps of the Australian state of South Australia for official use by the Department of the Chief Engineer.

E—Certain stamps of Bavaria, 1908 issue, have a large "E" overprint and were for the use of railway officials; the "E" signifies the German word for railway, "Eisenbahn."

EARLY IMPRESSION—A stamp that was printed early in the life of the plate, referring mainly to the stamps of the nineteenth century. When the design is clear and sharp as opposed to those printings from the same plate as it wears during the printing process.

E. B.—This overprint is found on stamps of the Australian state of South Australia and signifies official use by the Department of the Education Board.

EDWARDUS VII D. G. BRITT. OMN. REX F. D. IND. IMP.—This is an abbreviation for a Latin inscription found on certain stamps of Antigua. The inscription means 'Edward VII. By the Grace of God King of Greater Britain, Defender of the Faith, and Emperor of India."

EENDRAGT MAAKT MAGT.—This was the mottto of the South African Republic and is found on the stamp design immediately below the coat of arms. It means "Union makes Strength."

EFTERPORTO—This inscription is found on the postage due stamps of the Danish West Indies and refers to postage to be paid.

EGEO—This overprint is found on certain stamps of Italy and was for use in the Aegean Islands. The word Egeo is the Italian form for Aegean.

ELECTROTYPE—This is the finished copper or steel plated block which is an exact replica of an original die. The electro block is used in surface printing. One or more blocks of similar or different designs or stamps may be fastened together and one electrotype made of the pane or sheet of stamps.

EMBLEMS WATERMARK—This very interesting watermark is found on various stamps of Great Britain issued during 1856-1867. In the two upper corners are two roses, a shamrock in the lower left corner and a thistle in the lower right corner, indicating the United Kingdoms of England, Ireland and Scotland.

EMBOSSED—Sometimes stamps are issued with an embossed center, or a raised design in the center or other part of the design, thus having some part of the stamp design in relief.

EMP. OTTOMAN—This inscription is found on the stamps of Imperial Turkey, also known as the Ottoman Empire.

ENCASED POSTAGE STAMPS—Postage stamps which have been encased for use as fractional currency. This usually was done in an extreme emergency, such as our Civil War days and the great inflation in Germany after World War I. These stamps are quite sought after and very much prized by coin collectors. Some of the encasements are round metal frames with a mica face and back. The stamp is visible on the face and sometimes there was advertising on the back.

E. R. I.—This overprint is found on certain stamps of Transvaal and were used during the latter part of the Boer War. The initials are for "Edwardus Rex Imperator"—Edward King Emperor.

ESCUDO—A unit of currency of Spain and colonies until about 1872. 1,000 milesimas were equal to 1 escudo.

ESCUELAS—Many stamps of Venezuela show this word which means "schools" in Spanish. The stamps were used for postage as well as revenue purposes, and any revenue thus acquired was allocated for the schools in Venezuela.

ESSAY—When a stamp is proposed for issue, a design is usually prepared in a drawing form and submitted to the requesting authorities. This is considered an essay. It may also be in the form of a printed design sometimes in different colors but mostly in the original form as submitted by the artist.

ESTERO—This overprint in found on the stamps of imperial Italy and were for the use of the Italian offices in foreign countries prior to 1908. The word means "foreign."

F

FACSIMILE—Another word for fake. Sometimes there are reproductions of stamps made for souvenir sale and they are marked with the word "facsimile." These are not collector items any more than a counterfeit.

FAVOR'S EXPRESS—This was a private express company in the New England States whose service was mainly for the delivery of packages.

FELDPOST—This word is found on the stamps of Austria and certain stamps of Germany, etc., indicating postage stamps for use of the troops in the field or army postal stations.

FERNANDO POO—A spanish colony in the Gulf of Guinea.

FERRARY—The full name of one of the greatest stamp collectors of all time, M. La Renotiere Ferrary (Philipp von Ferrary), is not as well known as his last name. The Ferrary collections contained most of the world's great rarities of postage stamps.

FILLER—A unit of currency of old Hungary. 100 filler were equal to 1 korona.

FINE IMPRESSION—This term is usually used to indicate first printings or first impressions of stamps from copper or steel plates. These would be distinct impressions rather than a coarser or worn impression from the same plates at later dates.

FLAT PLATE PRINTING—Stamps printed on a flat bed press where there are no ridges in the gum as in the rotary press printings. One can usually measure or compare a used rotary press issue and a used flat plate printing issue and find that the flat plate is slightly smaller than the rotary issue. This is due to the fact that the rotary press printing process caused the paper to stretch just enough to be a bit larger.

FLORIN—This is a unit of value which is shown on some of the stamps of Hungary and Montenegro mostly during the nineteenth century. The Hungarian florin was divided into 100 kreutzer and the Montenegrin florin was divided into 100 novcica.

F. M.—This overprint is found on the 10¢ and 15¢ stamps of France from 1901-39 and means "Franchise Militaire."

F.N.F.L.—An overprint on various stamps of the French Colonial Empire meaning "Forces Navales Francaises Libres" or "Free French Naval Forces," World War II.

FOLUS—This is a unit of value in the Indian state of Faridkot prior to 1887. 1 folus was worth ¼ of 1 anna.

FOURNIER—This is the name of a most prolific stamp counterfeiter. His facsimile productions of old and sometimes rare stamps, flooded the countries of Europe and found their way to other countries before they were detected.

F. R.—These letters in script form are found on the breast of the eagle on the stamps of Prussia of 1861. They mean "Fredericus Rex," for King Frederick IV of Prussia.

F. R. P. S. L.—When these initials follow a stamp collector's name, it is to indicate the person is a "Fellow of the Royal Philatelic Society" of London, England.

FRAME INVERTED—See page 12 for illustrations and detailed explanation.

FRANC—This is a unit of value among several countries such as France and colonies, Belgium, etc. 100 centimes are equal to 1 franc.

FRANCO—This is a unit of value of the Dominican Republic during 1883-1885. 100 centimos was equal to 1 franco.

FRANCO BOLLO—This inscription is found on many stamps of the Italian states and means "Free Stamp."

FRANK—Instead of putting a postage stamp on an envelope, some people in political life and others through special permission may sign their names in the corner of the envelope, and this is considered a franking privilege.

FRANQUEO—This word is found on some of the stamps of Peru and means "postage."

FRANQUEO DEFICIENTE—This inscription found on stamps of Ecuador, Nicaragua, Paraguay and Salvador means "postage due."

FRANQUEO OFICIAL—This surcharge is found on certain stamps of Ecuador, Guatemala, etc. and means "official postage."

FREI DURCH ABLOSUNG Nr. 21—This inscription is found on the stamps of the German State of Prussia, 1903, indicating official postage.

FREI DURCH ABLOSUNG Nr. 16—This inscription is found on the stamps of the German State of Baden, 1905, indicating official postage.

FRIMAERKE—This word is found on the stamps of Norway issued prior to 1872 and means "free stamp."

FRIMAERKE K.G.L. POST—This inscription is found on the 2 rigsbanks-killing stamps of Denmark, 1851, and means "Free Stamps of the Royal Post."

FRIMARKE—The Swedish word for "free stamp."

FRIMERKI—The Icelandic word for "free stamp."

FT—This abbreviation is for the unit of value, the florin, and is found on certain high values of Hungary. It is the abbreviated form of the Hungarian spelling "forint."

F.T.T.—Italian stamps showing this overprint were used in the Free Territory of Trieste after World War II.

FUGITIVE INK—A stamp printed in a type of ink that will not stand cleaning or washing of the cancellation. Good examples of this are the stamps of Netherlands East Indies issued in 1933 to 1937, unwatermarked.

G

G—There were various stamps of the Cape of Good Hope which were overprinted with the letter "G" in quite a few different sizes and shapes. These stamps were for use in the territory of Griqualand, Africa, from 1874 to 1880.

GARTER—This is a watermark that is found on stamps of Great Britain prior to 1881. There are three different sizes of the Garter watermark: small, medium and large.

G.C.M.—An overprint in script or fancy letters, is one of the more common types used on the stamps of Mexico and means "Gobierno Constitucionalista Mexicano" or "Mexican Constitutional Government."

GENERAL COLLECTING—When a collector collects whatever stamps he can obtain from any country of the world or uses an album wherein spaces are allocated for some stamps of most countries of the world, this is referred to as general collecting.

GENERAL ISSUE—Ordinary postal issues of any country, not including commemorative issues or special printings for special events.

G. E. A.—This overprint is found on certain stamps of East Africa and Uganda which were for the use of the British troops occupying the territory of German East Africa during World War I.

GERUSALEMME—This is the Italian word for Jerusalem and is found overprinted on stamps of Italy for use of the Italian offices in Jerusalem.

G. F.—This is an overprint found on stamps of the Australian state of South Australia, indicating they were for the official use of the Gold Fields Department.

G. F. B.—This overprint is found on certain stamps of the island Kingdom of Tonga which were used for official purposes only. The initials mean "Gaue Faka Buleaga" or "On Government Service."

GIBBONS, STANLEY—While the name of Stanley Gibbons was probably the best known in stamp circles the world over during the nineteenth century, the firm name of Stanley Gibbons, Ltd. is today among the very top of the list of excellent stamp dealers of Great Britain and Europe and, of course, throughout the entire British Empire. The original firm was founded in 1856 and has prospered ever since. This is also the firm which produces the Stanley Gibbons Stamp Catalogues.

GOBIERNO—This overprint is found on certain stamps of Peru for official use, meaning "Government."

GOBIERNO CONSTITUCIONALISTA—This is an overprint found on many Mexican stamps during 1913-16 which was applied either by hand or printing press and was for use within restricted territory which was under the control of the Constitutional government.

GOURDE—This is a unit of value in the republic of Haiti. 1 gourde is equal to 100 centimes.

GOVT. PARCELS—This overprint is found on British stamps for the use of governmental departments when mailing parcels. They were discontinued in 1904.

G. P.—This overprint is found on certain stamps of the Australian state of South Australia indicating official use of the Government Printer prior to 1874.

G.P. DE M. This overprint is found on stamps of Mexico in 1916-17 and means "Gobierno Provisorio de Mexico" or "Provisional Government of Mexico."

G. P. O.—This abbreviation is known to mean "General Post Office" particularly in the British Empire.

GRANITE PAPER—A type of paper used by Switzerland and Austria in particular which can be readily identified by the minute pieces of variously colored silk threads embedded in the thin wove type paper. This paper has a blurred or mottled appearance.

GRANO—This is a unit of value which was used in the kingdom of Naples. 1 grano was $\frac{1}{100}$ of 1 ducat.

GREAT BARRIER ISLAND—This is an island sixty to seventy miles northeast of Auckland, New Zealand. It was here in 1897 that the idea of "pigeon post" mail was conceived by a man named W. Fricker. The stamps used were from a private manufacturer and were inscribed "Great Barrier Island," "Special Post" together with the face value. After the pigeons arrived in Auckland, New Zealand, with their messages, the messages were in turn mailed to the addressee in the usual manner. This private pigeon post was discontinued by order of the New Zealand government in 1899.

G. R. I.—This overprint is found on the stamps of certain German colonies as they were occupied by British troops during World War I. The letters stand for "Georgius Rex Imperator" or "George, King and Emperor."

GRILL—A small design or pattern impressed into the paper of a stamp with the intent to weaken the fiber so that the cancellation ink will be difficult or impossible to remove.

GROSCHEN—This was a unit of value within the North German Confederation and Germany until about 1874. 1 groschen was $\frac{1}{30}$ of 1 thaler.

GROSH—This was a unit of value of Albania and was the equivalent of 40 paras.

GROSION—This was a unit of value which appears on the stamps of Crete in 1899 as issued by the Russians for their governmental offices on Crete. 1 grosion was worth 4 metallik.

GROSSION—A unit of value in Albania. 1 grossion was worth 40 paras or 1 piastre.

GROTE—This was a unit of value in the former German state of Bremen and is shown on certain stamps of that state.

G. S.—This is an overprint found on certain stamps of the Australian state of South Australia prior to 1874 which were for the official use of the Government Storekeeper.

G. T.—This overprint is found on certain stamps of the Australian state of South Australia prior to 1874 which were for official use of the Department of Goolwa Tramways.

GT. PRE.—This overprint is found on certain stamps of Haiti in 1902 at the time of the new "provisional government." The abbreviation is for "Gouvernement Provisiore."

GUERCHE—A unit of currency of Abyssinia (Ethiopia) which is no longer used. 16 guerche was the equivalent of 1 taler, also 1 Maria Theresa taler.

GUIDE LINES—This usually refers to the perforation guide lines which are printed on the master sheets of stamps. These lines would divide a master sheet into the postoffice sheets of 50 or 100 subjects, depending on the size of the stamp.

GUILLOTINE PERFORATION—A perforation that is applied in one row of punches at a time or single line perforation. Sheets of stamps are perforated horizontally first, then passed through the machine for the vertical perforations.

GULDEN—A unit of currency in the Netherlands and its colonies. The Dutch gulden was the equivalent of 100 cents. Some of the old Austrian issues also

used this denomination. The Austrian gulden was the equivalent of 100 kreuzers.

GÜLTIG 9. ARMEE—This overprint is found on certain stamps of Romania indicating occupation by the German army during World War I, and that stamps so overprinted were valid for postage.

GUM—This is again another controversial point of stamp condition. Strictly speaking, it is the adhesive material applied to the backs of stamps for the purpose of attaching them to letters, parcels, etc. Many times the gum on the back of a stamp will be the determining factor as to whether or not a stamp is a reprint or an original issue.

GUM STAIN—There are a number of reasons why the gum on the back of a stamp will stain. The most noticeable stain is that which is referred to as tropical stain. This is a darkening of the gum, sometimes even discoloring the paper and causing the paper to crack. Humidity, salt air, etc., causes tropical stain. Many stamps of British Malaya, West Indies, etc., show this stain.

GUM WATERMARKS—This is a most unusual and rarely seen type of gum. In 1923 the Czechoslovakian government issued a commemorative set of stamps with the gum being applied in a quadrille style with the initials of the Republic "C.S.P." in the design of the gum.

G. W.—This overprint is found on certain stamps of the Cape of Good Hope during 1877 which were for use in Griqualand West.

H

H—This is an overprint which was found on stamps of the Australian state of South Australia prior to 1874 which were for the official use of Hospital authorities.

H. A.—This overprint is found on certain stamps of the Australian state of South Australia prior to 1874 which were for the use of official correspondence of the House of Assembly.

HABILITADO—This overprint is frequently found on the stamps of South and Central American countries, meaning "authorized." When stamps were so overprinted, they were usually of an obsolete design or value reactivated for use.

HAMILTON BANK NOTE CO.—This was a firm of printers and engravers in New York City which produced many stamps issued for certain South and Central American Republics, including the "Seebeck" issues of Ecuador, Nicaragua and Salvador.

HANDSTAMPED—This term can be applied to two categories of stamp collecting, because many times stamps were overprinted with a new value or to show military occupation by a country other than the stamp issuing country. The handstamp is also used to cancel a commemorative cover or envelope.

HARROW PERFORATION—A type of perforation which indicates that the entire sheet or pane of stamps was perforated at one time.

HELLER—A unit of currency in the old Austro-Hungarian Empire. 100 heller were equal to 1 krone. In German East Africa the heller was the low value and 100 heller were equal to 1 rupee.

HELVETIA—Another name for Switzerland.

HILL, SIR ROLAND—The name of the man who originated penny postage in England and who is often referred to as the father of the postage stamp.

HINGES—Stamp hinges are an absolute must for all collectors. A stamp hinge is no more than a small piece of glassine paper with a finely prepared, safe and tasteless gum applied to one side. The hinges of today are peelable and cannot hurt even the rarest stamp if properly used.

HONEYCOMB WATERMARK—This watermark design is found on stamps of Argentina and many other countries. It is called honeycomb because of its similarity in design to the pattern of a honeycomb.

HONI SOIT QUI MAL Y PENSE—This is the motto from the Arms of Great Britain and means "Evil be to him who evil thinks."

HRVATSKA—This is the native term for Croatia which was formerly a province of Hungary.

HUSSEY'S POST—This was a local post which operated in New York from 1854-1884. Many private postal labels were issued.

I

I. A.—This overprint is found on stamps of the Australian state of South Australia between 1868 and 1874 which were for official use of the Immigration Agent.

I. E.—This overprint is found on stamps of the Australian state of South Australia prior to 1874 which were for official use of the Interstate Estates.

I. E. F.—This overprint is found on stamps of India about 1913 which were for use of the British Indian troops, meaning "Indian Expeditionary Force."

I GILDI.—An overprint used during 1902-1903 in Iceland when certain stamps were overprinted to indicate they were valid for postage during the years listed.

IMPERFORATE—When a stamp has to be cut from a sheet or has no perforations, it is known as imperforate.

IMPRESSED WATERMARKS—This is a type of watermark that is impressed into the finished product rather than in the usual manner when the paper is still in the form of pulp. Good examples of the impressed watermark can easily be found on the stamps of Switzerland during 1862-1904.

IMPRIMATUR—This is a Latin word which translates to "let it be printed" and is used in connection with official approval of a proof impression of a sheet of stamps.

IMPUESTO DE GUERRA—This overprint is found on certain stamps of Puerto Rico under Spanish rule, 1898, and means "War Tax."

INDUSTRIELLE KRIEGSWIRT-SCHAFT—This overprint is found on Swiss stamps during 1918 to indicate that they were for use of the War Board of Trade.

INLAND REVENUE—These were stamps authorized by the department of the British government responsible for the collection of death duties, excise taxes, revenue stamps, etc.

INSTRUCCION—This word is found on certain stamps of Venezuela and means "instruction." They were issued for both postal and revenue purposes, and the revenue thus acquired was allocated to aid the state schools.

INTAGLIO—This is an Italian term applied to line-engraving and means "cut into." The lines of the design are cut into the plate.

INVERTED CENTER—This expression is used to indicate a stamp with the central part of the design printed upside down.

INVERTED SURCHARGE—This expression is used to indicate an overprint or surcharge which is upside down in relation to the normal stamp.

I. R. OFFICIAL—This overprint is found on certain stamps of Great Britain which were for use of the Board of Inland Revenue from 1882-1904.

I. S.—This overprint is found on stamps of the Australian state of South Australia prior to 1874 which were for official use of the Inspector of Sheep.

ISOLE JONIE—This overprint indicates the Italian occupation of the Ionian Islands during World War II.

ITA KARJALA—This overprint indicates the Finnish occupation of Russian Karelia, 1941.

J

JAMHURI—This overprint is found on stamps of Zanzibar, etc. and means "Republic."

JORNAES—This inscription is found on some stamps of Portugal and also overprinted on stamps of Mozambique which were for use on packages of printed matter. The word means "Journal."

JOURNAUX—This is the French rendition of the word "Journals" and was used on stamps issued in 1868.

JUAN FERNANDEZ ISLANDS—This name applies to a group of three volcanic islands in the Pacific Ocean some 400 miles west of Chile. In 1910 the words "Juan Fernandez Islands" were overprinted on some Chilean stamps and were for use in Chile as well as the Islands.

K

KAISERLICHE KONIGLICHE OSTER-REICHISCHE POST—This is an inscription found on the commemorative stamps of Austria in 1908, 1910, and the regular issue of 1916 and means "Imperial Royal Austrian Post."

KARLSFOND—This inscription is found on certain stamps of Austria and Bosnia and means "Charles Fund" for charity.

KARNTEN ABSTIMMUNG—This overprint is found on certain stamps of the Austrian Republic and means "Plebicite for Carinthia."

K. C.—This inscription is found on many of the early stamps of the kingdom of Serbia and means "Princely Serbian Post."

KEMAHKOTAAN—This overprint is found on certain stamps of the Malay state of Johore and means "coronation."

KENETA—This is the Hawaiian spelling of the word "cents" and is found on many of the stamps of the kingdom of Hawaii prior to 1894.

KING EDWARD VII LAND—This overprint is found on the Edward VII one-penny stamps of New Zealand which were for use of the Shackleton Expedition in 1907-1909 during exploration of the southern Antarctic region.

KINGSTON RELIEF FUND—This overprint and surcharge is found on the two-penny stamps of Barbados and was issued in 1907 with the surcharge value going to the fund for the relief of Jamaica after a most disastrous earthquake.

K.K.H.M.—These initials stand for "Kaiserliche-Konigliche Handels-Ministerium" and are found as a watermark in the Austrian stamps of 1850. It is considered a papermaker's watermark and is found only in the hand-made paper.

KNTAN—This overprint is found on many stamps of Imperial Russia which were for use of Russian post offices in China.

KOPEC—This is a unit of value and is found on the stamps of Imperial Russia, Poland, and the early issues of the Duchy of Finland. 1 kopec was 1/100 of a ruble.

KORONA—This was a unit of value of Hungary. 1 korona was worth 100 filler.

KOZTARSASAG—This overprint is found on many Hungarian stamps after World War I and means "Republic."

KPHTH—This is the Greek spelling for Crete and is shown on the Cretan stamps.

KRAN—A unit of currency of old Persia. 1 kran was the equivalent of 20 chahis.

KREUZER—This was a unit of currency in several German states prior to World War I, also used in early Austria and Hungary. Many currency changes were adopted and the various values differed.

KRONA—This is a unit of value of Sweden and Iceland. The Icelandic krona contains 100 aur, and the Swedish krona contains 100 ore.

K.U.K. FELDPOST—This inscription is found on the military stamps of Austria as used by Austrian troops as well as on stamps overprinted by Austria for the occupation of Italy during World War I.

K.u.K. MILITAR POST—This inscription is found on the military stamps of the Austro-Hungarian Empire. It means "Kaiserliche und Konigliche" in reference to the Austrian emperor being emperor of Austria and king of Hungary.

L

L. A.—This overprint is found on certain stamps of the Australian state of South Australia for the official use of the Department of the Lunatic Asylum.

LADY McLEOD—This was the name of a ship owned by David Boyce in 1847. Letters carried aboard the Lady McLeod were prepared for delivery by the use of a fascinating little local stamp. The range of delivery of such mail was limited to Trinidad, Port of Spain, etc. in the West Indies.

LAID PAPER—Stamps have been printed on two kinds of laid paper, vertical and horizontal. When the paper pulp is being processed into paper it is run over a type of gauze in which the lines are set close together either in horizontal or vertical format. When held to the light these lines are usually very distinct.

LAUREATED—It has long been considered, especially in Europe, that while a crown of jewels may be obtained by election or by heredity, a crown of laurel is only won by the abilities and the strength of the victor. Few stamps portray national rulers wreathed with laurel. Among the most readily recognized are the issues of New South Wales: during 1850 to 1863 with Queen Victoria, and the issues of France from 1862 to 1870 with Napoleon III.

L. C.—This overprint is found on certain stamps of the Australian state of South Australia which were for the official use of the Legislative Council.

LEPTON—This is a unit of currency in Greece and in Crete. 100 lepton is equal to 1 drachma.

LEU—This is a unit of currency in Romania. 1 leu contains 100 bani.

LEVA—This is a unit of value in Bulgaria. 1 leva contains 100 stotinki.

LINE ENGRAVING—Stamps were first printed by this process, whereby an engraver cuts the artist's design into a soft steel die which is hardened and rolled over a soft steel plate to transfer the design. A series of transfers are made from the engraved die which in turn form the plate; ink is rolled on the plate filling every engraved cut with ink. The plate is wiped clean, then burnished; and by the pressure of the printing roller the ink-filled cuts are squeezed onto damp paper giving clear image of engraved design.

LITHOGRAPHY—See offset printing page 216.

L. L.—This overprint is found on certain stamps of the Australian state of South Australia for the official correspondence of the Legislative Library.

LOSEN—This word is found on the postage due stamps of Sweden of 1874-1877.

L. T.—This overprint is found on certain stamps of the Australian state of South Australia which were for the official use of the Land Titles Department.

M

M—This overprint is found on certain stamps of the Australian state of South

Australia which were for the official use of the Military Department.

M. A.—This overprint is found on certain stamps of the republic of Argentina in 1913 for use of the Ministry of Agriculture.

MAGYAR—This is the Hungarian word for Hungary and is found in different presentations, such as Magyarorazag, meaning "State of Hungary," and Magyar Kir Posta, meaning "Hungarian Post Services," etc.

MAI GT. PRE. 1902—This overprint is found on certain stamps of Haiti and were applied by handstamp for the then provisional government.

M. A. L.—This overprint was used by the British forces in former Italian colonial areas of East and North Africa. The initials mean "Military Authority Lire."

MALTESE CROSS—There are several versions of the shape of the Maltese Cross. They vary as used for stamp designs, as watermark designs, and also as cancellation designs. The Maltese Cross dates from the era of the Crusaders.

MARK—This was a unit of value in Germany and certain German states. 100 pfennig equaled 1 mark.

MARKKA—This is a unit of value in Finland. 1 markka is the equivalent of 100 pennia.

MARTIN'S CITY POST—This was a local post in Charleston, South Carolina, in 1858.

MATRIX—This is the name of the original die from which stamps are made. It is also a general die from which stamps of the same design but different values are made.

MAXIMUM CARD—A true maximum card is a postcard which has a picture on one side that has been reproduced in a postage stamp design. A stamp with that same design is applied to the *picture side* of the card and cancelled.

M. B.—This overprint is found on certain stamps of the Australian state of South Australia for use of official correspondence of the Marine Board.

M. E. F.—This overprint is indicative of the British Middle East Forces.

MERRY WIDOW—This gay name was given to the design of the United States special delivery stamp of 1908. The design of Mercury's helmet seemed apropos to the tune of the day from the show "The Merry Widow," and many stylishly dressed ladies of that day wore hats in somewhat similar design.

M. G.—This overprint is found on certain stamps of the republic of Argentina in 1913 for official use of the War Department. The initials stand for "Ministerio de Guerra."

M. H.—This overprint is found on certain stamps of the republic of Argentina in 1913 for the Ministry of Finance. The initials stand for "Ministerio de Hacienda."

M. I.—This overprint is found on certain stamps of the republic of Argentina in 1913 for official use of the Ministry of Interior. The initials stand for "Ministerio del Interior."

MILESIMO—This is a unit of value of Uruguay. 1 milesimo is $\frac{1}{1000}$ of 1 peso.

MILLIEME—This is a unit of value of Egypt and Sudan. 10 milliemes are the equivalent of 1 piastre.

MILLIMETRE—This is the name of $\frac{1}{1000}$ part of a meter which is of the metric measurement system.

MINT—When a stamp is referred to as "mint," it is with full gum on the back and, of course, uncancelled. If the stamp was issued without gum, it would mean being uncancelled.

MIRANDA, APOTESOIS DE—In 1896 Venezuela issued a set of map stamps to commemorate the 80th anniversary of the death of General Miranda, the father of the Venezuelan Republic.

MIXED PERFORATION—This term applies to stamps perforated with entirely different holes on the sides or the top and bottom. Good examples of this type of perforation is in the South Africa war issue of 1942-44 where there are roulette perforations and round perforations on the same stamp.

M. J. I.—This overprint is found on certain stamps of the republic of Argentina in 1913. The stamps were for the official use of the Ministry of Justice and Education. The initials stand for "Ministerio de Justicia y Instruccion."

M. M.—This overprint is found on certain stamps of the republic of Argentina in 1913 for official use of the Navy Department. The initials stand for "Ministerio de Marina."

MOIRE—This is a type of security printing which is seldom used these days. It consists usually of a neat type of pattern, somewhat like a burelage, and is found usually on the backs of stamps being thus protected.

MON—This was a unit of currency of early Japan. The first stamps of Japan were issued in the mon denominations. 100 mon were equal to 1 sen.

MOON—This was a unit of currency in the kingdom of Korea.

M. O. P.—This overprint is found on certain stamps of the republic of Argentina in 1913 for the official use of the Ministry of Public Works. The initials stand for "Ministerio de Obras Publicas."

MOURNING STAMP—A mourning stamp should not be confused with a stamp issued in honor or commemoration of an anniversary of a death. A good example of a mourning stamp is the black bordered Belgian stamps showing the portrait of Queen Astrid who was killed in an automobile accident in 1935.

M. Q. E.—These initials, an abbreviation for the colony of Martinique, were overprinted on the 20¢ general issue of French colonial stamps for provisional use within Martinique.

M. R.—This overprint is found on certain stamps of the Australian state of South Australia for the official use of the Manager of Railways prior to 1874.

M. R. C.—This overprint is found on certain stamps of the Argentine Republic in 1913 for the official use of the Ministry of Foreign Affairs and Religion. The initials stand for "Ministerio de Relaciones y Culto."

M. R. G.—This overprint is found on certain stamps of the Australian state of South Australia for the official use of the Department of Main Roads, Gambierton.

MUESTRA—This is the Spanish word for pattern or specimen.

MULREADY ENVELOPE—William Mulready was the well known English artist who designed the first postal envelopes of Great Britain known as the 1 penny and the 2 penny Mulready envelopes.

MULTA—This word appears on several issues of stamps from South American countries (Chile, Costa Rica, etc.) and means "postage due."

MULTIPLE WATERMARK—This should not be confused with a continuous watermark because a multiple watermark shows a repeat of the same design many times, whereas a continuous watermark is one which is continuous of the inscription such as the English manuscript type which reads "halfpenny".

M.V.i.R.—This overprint is found on various stamps of Germany and Romania and means "Military Administration of Romania." The initials stand for "Militar Verwaltung in Rumanien," during World War I.

N

NADRUK—In the Dutch language this word means "reprint." It is found on the back of most of the reprints of the stamps of the 1852 issue for the Netherlands.

NATIVE PAPER—Paper made in the Orient by natives. This type of paper was made in Japan and in some of the Indian Native States. The Japanese type is of a tough and fibrous nature, usually either laid or wove; the Indian type is thicker.

NE PAS LIVRER LE DIMANCHE—This inscription is found at the base of Belgian stamps issued from 1893-1915 and means "do not deliver Sunday" in French.

NEU-GROSCHEN—This was a unit of value in Saxony and was $\frac{1}{30}$ part of the thaler.

NEW GRANADA—This was the name of the present republic of Colombia prior to 1862.

N. F.—This overprint is found on some of the stamps of the Nyasaland Protectorate in 1917 for use in the former territory of German East Africa occupied by British forces during World War I and means "Nyasaland Forces."

N. G. R.—These perforated letters are found on certain stamps of Natal which were used for official correspondence of the Natal Government Railways.

NIET BESTELLEN OP ZONDAG—This inscription is found on the stamps of Belgium from 1893-1915 and means "not to be delivered on Sunday" in Flemish.

NOVCIC—This was a unit of value in the kingdom of Montenegro prior to 1902. 100 novcica were the equivalent of 1 florin.

N. S. B.—These initials are found on various stamps of the General French colonial issue for use in the colony of Nossi-be.

N. T.—This overprint is found on certain stamps of the Australian state of South Australia prior to 1874 for the official correspondence of the Department of the Northern Territory.

O

O. A.—This overprint is found on certain stamps of the Australian state of South Australia between 1868-1874 for the official use of the Department of the Official Assignee.

O. B.—This overprint is found on the stamps of the Philippine Islands in various sizes and means "Official Business."

OCCUPATION STAMPS—During the past years since postage stamps were issued, there have been many types of occupation stamps. This is simply a group of postage stamps that have been issued or overprinted or surcharged by an occupying power to indicate to the population that they are now under the authority of the occupying country.

ODONTOMETRE—This is the French word or expression for perforation gauge.

OFFSET PRINTING—In this lithographic printing process the basic rule applies that grease and water repel each other. In the offset process the stamp design is photographed by a reproduction camera, then a brilliant light is used to transfer the image from the negative to a sensitized metal plate. An emulsion is wiped on, thus fixing the image to the plate. The photo-engraved plate is then wrapped around a cylinder ready to transfer the image to the rubber printing blanket which in turn prints the image on the paper.

O. G.—This is an abbreviation generally used in philatelic circles meaning "original gum" on the back of the stamp.

O.H.B.M.S.—This overprint means "On His Brittanic Majesty's Service."

O.H.E.M.S.—This overprint means "On His Exalted Majesty's Service." (Egypt)

O. H. H. S.—This overprint is found on certain stamps of Egypt which were for official use and means "On His Highness' Service."

O.H.M.S.—This overprint is found on certain stamps of the Somaliland Protectorate for official use, meaning "On His Majesty's Service."

"O.M.F."—This overprint is found on certain stamps of France for use in Syria and means "Occupation Militaire Francaise."

ON H. M. S.—This overprint is found on certain stamps of India for official use and means "On Her, (or His) Majesty's Service."

ON K.D.S.—This overprint is found on certain official stamps of the Indian state of Kishengarh and means "On Kishengarh Durbar Service."

ON S. S. S.—This overprint is found on certain stamps of the Indian state of

Sirmoor for official use and means "On Sirmoor State Service."

O. P. S. O.—This overprint is found on certain stamps of New Zealand for official use of the Post Office Department and means "On Public Service Only."

ORE—This is a unit of value expressed on many stamps of Norway, Sweden, and Denmark. 100 ore is the equivalent of 1 krone.

ORIGINAL GUM—A mint stamp is that stamp which has the original gum on the back as applied in the manufacturing process. Stamps of the 19th or early 20th century with their original gum are usually easy to distinguish from reprints made at a later date, or even a stamp which has been re-gummed.

ORTS POST—This inscription is found on the stamps of Zurich of 1850 as well as the 2½ rappen stamp of Switzerland. The words are German and mean "Local Post."

O. S.—This overprint is found on many stamps of the Australian States intended for official correspondence and means "On Service."

"O.M.F."—This overprint is found on certain stamps of New Britain and means "Official Service George Rex Imperator." The overprint was applied to the former German colonial stamps of German New Guinea.

O. S. G. S.—This overprint is found on certain stamps of Sudan for official correspondence and means "On Sudan Government Service."

OSTLAND—This overprint is found on the stamps of Hitler Germany to indicate German military occupation of Russia.

OVERPRINT—An additional printing on the face of the stamp after it is originally printed and completed. An overprint does not change the value as does a surcharge. However, an overprint may be combined with a surcharge on one stamp.

OXIDIZED COLOR—The oxidation of color can ruin a stamp from a point of value as well as appearance. The hardest hit of all colors are the orange and orange-brown shades. The orange turns brownish and the orange-brown turns a poor blackish-brown. This is often caused by sulphur in the paper of an album page or the envelope on which it was used or the paper of the stamp itself; in some cases, certain tropical conditions will also bring about oxidation.

P

P—This overprint is found on certain stamps of the Australian state of South Australia between 1868 and 1874, used on official correspondence of the department dealing with Police affairs.

P—This overprint together with a star and crescent, all within an oval, is found on certain stamps of the Strait Settlements for use in the Malay state of Perak.

P. A.—This overprint is found on certain stamps of the Australian state of South Australia prior to 1874 for official correspondence of the Protector of Aborigines.

PAISA—This is a unit of value found on certain states of India and related areas. One paisa was equivalent to one quarter anna.

PAPER—All stamp collectors are interested in paper for the obvious reason that many varieties of postage stamps are due to the paper upon which they are printed. While linen and cotton rag content make a better grade of paper, there are many other ingredients that have been used over the years to make different grades of paper such as wood, straw, cereal straws, mulberry bark, khoi, bamboo, jute, etc.

PAPERMAKER'S WATERMARKS—These are the trademarks of certain paper manufacturers and could form a most interesting collection for the diligent and tireless searcher. There are many of them, and they were used as an identification more than anything else. They are usually found on the edges or borders of the sheets of paper supplied to the government printing offices of various countries. Sometimes the papermaker's watermark was so placed that some stamps received part of the design during the printing process.

PAQUEBOT—This word is usually found as a postal mark on any mail posted at sea.

PARA—This was a unit of value within certain countries of the Near East, especially Turkey. Stamps of Austria, Germany, France, etc. were surcharged and overprinted in this currency for use in their respective offices in Turkey. 40 paras were the equivalent of 1 piaster.

PARAPHE—While we seldom hear this word anymore, it was used to indicate a broad manuscript or flourish script such as was applied to old time signatures. This script is found on certain stamps of Cuba particularly.

PART PERFORATED—In the case of coil stamps or certain types of booklet panes, part perforation is as originally issued. There are, however, errors during perforation processes which cause a stamp or a group of stamps to receive only part of their regular perforation. This is also sometimes known as "imperforate between."

PATACA—This is a unit of value in Portuguese colonies of Macao and Timor. 1 pataca is worth 100 avos.

PELURE PAPER—A hard and tough transparent paper, very thin, upon which the stamps of certain countries have been printed.

PEN-CANCELLED—Pen-cancelled more often than not, indicated the stamp has been used for purposes other than postal use. It does indicate a use in fiscal and revenue departments, although there are exceptions such as manuscript cancels, etc.

PENI—The penny values used in the kingdom of Tonga.

PENNI—This is a unit of value in Finland. 100 pennia are the equivalent of 1 mark.

PERCE EN ARC—A familiar type of roulette perforation in a semi-circular pierced arc design.

PERCE EN CROIX—This is another type of roulette perforation in the form of cuts or indentations as a row of XXXX's.

PERCE EN LIGNES—This is perhaps the most noticeable type of roulette perforation used in the manufacture of postage stamps, being a series of straight line indentations or cuts.

PERCE EN LOSANGES—This type of roulette perforations show the indentations or cuts in the form of a series of small diamond shapes.

PERCE EN POINTS—The very small pin-point type of perforation holes.

PERCE EN SCIE—Most stamp collectors know this to be a saw-tooth type of roulette perforation and be quite common. It is often found on the German inflation stamps of the 1923 era.

PERCE EN SERPENTINE—This type of roulette perforation is very noticeable as a wavy line which is found particularly on the stamps of early Finland.

PERFORATION—This one word has a great fascination for the stamp collector because, as with watermarks, the perforations very often mean a great deal of difference in the value of the issue of postage stamps. Actually, perforation is the general name to the many types, styles, or designs of the holes between the stamps for their easy separation. A stamp collector always uses a perforation gauge to determine the gauge of the perfs on his stamp.

PERFORATION GAUGE—Because there are so many variations of perforations which can mean many dollars difference in value, every stamp collector should have a perforation gauge. This applies to the beginner, the old timer, the general collector and in particular, the specialist.

PERPER—A unit of value in the kingdom of Montenegro. 1 perper was worth 100 paras.

PESA—This was a unit of value of the former German colony of German East Africa prior to 1900. 1 pesa was worth 1/64 of 1 rupee.

PESETA—This is a unit of value of Spain and colonies and post offices. 1 peseta is worth 100 centimos.

PESO—This is a unit of value of many Spanish speaking countries of South and Central America and is usually worth 100 centavos.

P. G. S.—This overprint is found on certain stamps of the Strait Settlements and means "Perak Government Service."

PIASTRE—This was a unit of value in the kingdom of Romania prior to 1868. 1 piastre was worth 40 parale.

PIASTRE—This is a unit of value as found in certain countries of the Near East, such as Turkey, Crete, Cyprus, the Sudan, etc. 1 piastre is usually worth 40 paras.

PICE—This is a unit of value which is in use even today in certain parts of India. 4 pice are equal to 1 anna.

PIE—This is a unit of value in certain states of India. 12 pies are equal to 1 anna.

PIN PERFORATION—See Perce en points.

PIGEON POST—This usually refers to the carrier pigeon post between Great Barrier Island and Auckland, New Zealand, which was operated as a private post, suppressed by the New Zealand postal authorities in 1899.

PLATE NUMBER—This refers to the official number assigned to a particular plate from which stamps are printed. In the U.S.A. a great many collectors collect plate number blocks of 6 stamps when printed by flat plate process, or plate blocks of 4 when printed by rotary press process. The plate numbers are on the margin or selvage of a sheet, and sometimes there are two numbers in different colors to indicate the color plate number. In the case of the U.S.A. flag series of the overrun countries, in 1943-44, the country name was used instead of a plate number.

PLATE PROOF—This term should not be confused with a die proof. A plate proof is simply printer's proof from the finished plate; a die proof is an impression which is taken from the die which was used in making the plate.

POCZTA POLSKA—This inscription is found on the stamps of Poland, Germany, and Austria and means "Polish Post."

POHJOIS INKERI—This is the native expression of North Ingermanland which was a very controversial territory in Northern Russia in 1920.

POON—This was a unit of value in the kingdom of Korea between 1895 and 1900. 5 poon were the equivalent of 1 cheun.

PORTEADO A. RECEBER—This inscription is shown on the parcel post stamps of Peru and means "Postage for Conveyance."

PORTO—This word is found on the postage due stamps of Austria and the Austrian Levant and means "postage."

PORTOMAERKE—This inscription is found on the postage due stamps of the Danish West Indies and Norway.

POSCHTA—This is the Russian word for post.

POSTAGE CURRENCY—This term usually applies to those small pieces of fractional currency issued by the U.S. government in 1862-63 during the early part of the Civil War. They were issued to alleviate the shortage of small coins, and had postage stamps as designs to indicate the value. A five cent note showed the 5¢ brown Jefferson regular postage stamp, the 50¢ note showed five of the 10¢ green Washington regular postage stamp. The denominations issued were 5¢, 10¢, 25¢, 50¢.

POSTE ESTENSI—This inscription is found on certain stamps of Modena and means "Post of the House of Este." The rulers of the Duchy of Modena were of the House of Este.

POSTE KHEDEVIE EGIZIANE—This inscription is found on certain stamps of Egypt between 1872 and 1875 and means "Khedival Egyptian Post."

POSTE PERSANE—This inscription is shown on the stamps of Persia between 1891 and 1898 and means "Persian Post." After 1898 the inscription was changed to the plural "Postes Persanes."

POSTES OTTOMANES—This inscription is found on the stamps of the Ottoman Empire (Turkey) and means "Ottoman Post."

POSTGEBIET OB. OST.—This overprint is found on certain stamps of Germany during World War I for use in the occupied areas of the Eastern command. The overprint means "Postal Areas of the Eastern Commander in Chief" and was used mainly in the Lithuanian area.

POST HORN—The design of a post horn is very often found in the watermark and featured designs of the stamps of the nineteenth century, particularly in Central Europe.

POSTMARK—This is simply an identifying mark of obliteration which cancels the stamp. It is also used to identify the backstamp on a cover.

POST TENEBRAS LUX—This is the motto of the Swiss Canton of Geneva and is shown above the coat of arms on its first stamp; the meaning is "After Darkness, Light."

POSTZEGEL—This inscription is found on the early stamps of the Netherlands and certain stamps of the South African Republic. It is the Dutch expression for "postage stamps."

P. P.—This postmark is often found on nineteenth century correspondence. The initials mean "Poste Paye" or "postage paid."

P. R.—These initials are found as a watermark on certain stamps of the kingdom of Romania. They stand for "Posta Romania" or "Romanian Post."

PRIR—A surcharge found on the stamps of Iceland issued in 1897 meaning "three."

PRO JUVENTUTE—This inscription is found on the semi-postal stamps of Switzerland and means "for youth." The extra funds derived from the sales of the stamps were to be used for a health protection program for children.

PROVISIONAL ISSUE—Stamps that were surcharged to be worth a different value than their original face value at the time of issue. A classic example of a provisional surcharge is the one from St. Vincent. The 4d is surcharged over the original one shilling value because of a shortage of the 4d values and an overabundance of the shilling value.

PROVISORIO—This inscription is found on a stamp of Bolivia, five cent value, originally issued as a revenue stamp but when overprinted, it was then available for postal use in 1893; it means "provisional."

P. S.—This overprint is found on certain stamps of the Australian state of South Australia during 1868 to 1874 for the official use on correspondence of the Private Secretary.

PUNCH PERFORATIONS—This expression is used when one is referring to stamps from any part of the world that have initials or words perforated into the design. This practice was mainly instituted to prevent pilferage and employee use of a business firm's stock of stamps.

PUTTAN—This was a unit of value in the Indian Native State of Cochin. 1 puttan was worth about 1 anna.

P. W.—This overprint is found on certain stamps of the Australian state of South Australia during 1868 to 1874 for the official use of the Public Works Department.

PYNUNG—This was a unit of value which was expressed in native characters on the first stamps of Siam. 1 pynung was worth 2 atts.

Q

QINT—This was a unit of value in Albania in 1913. 100 qintar equaled 1 franc.

QUADRILLE RULED PAGES—This is nothing more than extra sheets for a looseleaf album binder with a fine quadrille ruled series of lines, like graph paper, to aid in placing the stamps and the lettering in a straight position.

QUATREFOILS—A scarce watermark design. Several countries have used this design. See Whitman Watermark #126.

QUATTRINI—This was a unit of value usually abbreviated to "quatte" and is found on certain stamps of the Italian state of Tuscany. 60 quattrini were worth 1 lira.

QUETZAL—This is a sacred bird of Guatemala and is often seen as the subject of the stamp designs of that country. Tradition has a story that at the time of the murder of a revered native ruler at the hands of the conquistadors of Spain, a spurt of blood from the king fell upon the breast of the quetzal bird. From that day to this, no one has seen a quetzal bird without the red breast.

R

R—The initial "R" is the internationally recognized postal abbreviation for the word "registration" or "registered."

R—This overprint is found on certain stamps of the French colonial general issue and was for use in the Reunion Islands prior to 1891.

RAPPEN—This was a unit of value found on the early stamps of Switzerland. 100 rappen equaled 1 franc.

RAWDON, WRIGHT, HATCH & EDSON—This was the name of the New York printing firm, manufacturers of the United States 1847 stamps. Together with several other firms they formed the American Bank Note Company in 1858.

RAYON—This inscription is found on certain stamps of Switzerland between 1850-54 and refers to the radius wherein the postal fee for delivery charges was paid by the postage stamps.

R. B.—This overprint is found on certain stamps of the Australian state of South Australia prior to 1874 for the official use of the Road Board Department.

R. B. S.—These initials are found on the first 4 skilling stamps of Denmark and mean "rigsbank skilling." 96 rigsbank skilling were equivalent to 1 rigsbank daler.

REAL—This was the unit of value found on the early stamps of Spain and colonies and certain Southern and Central American countries. 8 reals were worth 1 peso; 4 Spanish reales were worth 1 peseta.

REAL M. C.—This was a unit of value meaning "moneda corriente" or "current money" and is found on the first stamp of Corrientes.

REAL PLATA FUERTE—This was a monetary value expression found on certain early stamps of the Philippine Islands and Cuba. It means "coin silver" rather than "paper currency."

RECONSTRUCTED PLATE—When a collector or a specialist reconstructs a plate of stamps it is also referred to as just plain "plated." Many collectors have "plated" certain of the early stamps of Great Britain as they were easily reconstructed from the corner letters which are different on each stamp in the sheet. By knowing the layout of the original sheet, the collector assembles one stamp of each set of letters and thus can reconstruct a sheet of stamps of a given denomination.

RECUTTING—This term should be applied to the alteration required to a die or a plate.

REDRAWN—When a stamp design has been redrawn it usually means that some slight change or modification was decided upon which necessitated the engraving of a new die.

RE-ENGRAVED—There have been times when dies and plates have been strengthened or re-engraved or recut to improve the production of the design of the stamp. The finished impression which has been obtained after recutting is often referred to as having been re-engraved.

REGATUL PTT ROMANIEI—This overprint in a circle is found on stamps of Hungary for the use of the occupying troops of Romania during World War I.

REGNO D'ITALIA VENEZIA GIULIA—This overprint by the Italian military authorities is found on certain stamps of imperial Austria during the occupation of Trieste and Venezia Giulia in 1918.

REICHSPOST—This inscription is found on the stamps of Germany prior to 1902 and means "Imperial Post."

REIS—This was a unit of value in Portugal and Brazil. 1,000 reis were equal to 1 millreis.

RE-ISSUE—This term applies to any stamp or set of stamps of which fresh printings have been made. There is usually some slight difference which will pinpoint them as being re-issues, such as shade of color or some other characteristic.

REMAINDERS—This usually refers to the unsold, remaining stock of any given commemorative issue or regular postage series of values which are no longer to be issued to the public by any government or by the government of issue. The stamps are genuine, but many have been demonetized, or the country may have gone through a serious inflation which nullified the value, or a change of government affected the use of these stamps. A modern example is the discovery in Italy of thousands of sheets of stamps used by the former imperial government of Italy in its offices abroad; all remainders were obsolete and demonetized, and the stamps were earmarked for destruction.

REPRINTS—This term means the stamps that have been reprinted from original plates or dies, usually after the post office selling of the original stamps had stopped. Reprints are only souvenirs or specimens of design.

REPUBLICA ORIENTAL—The complete title of the republic of Uruguay is "Republica Oriental del Uruguay." The words mean "Eastern Republic" and have been a part of the name of the country since 1830.

RE-TOUCHING—This refers to only minor touch-up work done to a die or a plate.

RESMI—This is an overprint or inscription on Turkish stamps and means "official."

REVENUE STAMPS—These stamps are not available for postal duties as they were issued primarily for fiscal purposes.

R. F.—These initials stand for "Republic France" and are found on many stamps of the French Colonial Empire.

R. G.—This overprint is found on certain stamps of the Australian state of South Australia prior to 1874 for the official use of the Registrar General.

R. H.—These initials are found in the watermark of the Haitian stamps of 1898 and mean "Republic D'Haiti."

R. H. OFFICIAL—This overprint is found on certain stamps of Great Britain in 1902 for use of the official correspondence of the Royal Household; they are quite rare.

RIALTAR SEALADAC na HEIREANN—This overprint means "Provisional Irish Government."

RIBBED PAPER—This type of paper has a smooth side and a slightly "ribbed" side with ridges and furrows.

RIKSDALER—This was a unit of value in Sweden prior to 1878. The original riksdaler was the equivalent of 48 skillingbanco.

RIN—This is a unit of value shown on certain stamps of Japan. 10 rin were worth 1 sen.

R. I. S.—These initials stand for the "Republic of Indonesia Serikat."

R. M.—These initials are found in a watermark of certain stamps of Mexico, 1896-97, and stand for "Republica Mexico."

R. O.—This overprint is found on certain stamps of Turkey for use in Eastern Roumelia. The letters mean "Roumelie Orientale."

ROMANA, ZONA de OCCUPATIE—This overprint was used on Hungarian stamps overprinted by Romanian occupational forces in 1919.

ROSBACK—The F. P. Rosback Company of Benton Harbor, Michigan, installed a perforating machine in Washington, D. C., in which the one-cent stamps of 1919 were perforated 12½ to identify them from the regular issue of the day. They are very popular United States items and eagerly sought after by collectors.

ROUGH IMPRESSION—This applies to a stamp which shows a rough and inferior impression of the design. It can also determine the location of printing a given issue if there were two or more printing plants doing the work.

ROUGH PERFORATION—When a stamp has a ragged or rough look around the perforated edges.

ROULETTE PERFORATION—When a stamp is perforated by roulette method there are no holes punched through the paper. There are only slits or indentations in assorted styles. Sometimes these slits or indentations are made in color, during the printing of the stamps.

R. P. R.—This overprint is found on certain stamps of Romania and means "Romanian Peoples' Republic."

RUBLE—This is a unit of value in both Imperial and Communist Russia. 1 ruble is worth 100 kopecks.

RUPEE—This is a unit of value in India, Ceylon, Mauritius, Seychelles, Zanzibar, etc. 1 rupee is usually worth 16 annas.

RUPIA—This was a unit of value in Portuguese India. 1 rupia was worth 16 tangas.

RUPIE—This was a unit of value in German East Africa up to 1895. 1 rupie was worth 64 pesas, and after 1895 it was worth 100 heller.

RUSH MILLS—This is the name of the paper mills in North Hampden, England; the manufacturer of the paper used for the first British stamps.

R. W. H. E.—These initials stand for the firm of Rawdon, Wright, Hatch and Edson of New York, the engravers and printers of the first United States stamp of 1847. The initials are found at the bottom of these designs in very small letters.

S

S—Certain stamps of the Straits Settlements are found with this overprint, either alone or with stars and crescents, indicating use in the state of Selangor.

S—This overprint is found on certain stamps of the Australian state of South Australia prior to 1874 for the official correspondence of the Sheriff for the colony.

S. A.—These initials, perforated into the design of the stamp, indicated official correspondence of the state of South Australia.

SAARSTAT EIREANN—This expression means "Irish Free State."

SADIPO SATISE—Overprint South Africa; South African Tercentenary International Stamp Exhibition.

SAFETY PAPER—There were several types of so-called safety paper used over the years in the manufacture of postage stamps. The prime reason was to eliminate the possibility of anyone removing the cancellation and being able to re-use the stamp for its face value.

SALUNG—This was a unit of value of the old kingdom of Siam and was worth about ¼ of 1 tical.

SANAR—This was a unit of value found on the stamp of the older issue of Afghanistan. 6 sanar were worth 1 rupee.

SATANG—This is a unit of value in Siam, 100 satangs equal 1 tical.

S. C.—This overprint is found on certain stamps of the Australian state of South Australia prior to 1874 for the official use of the Supreme Court.

SCH—This abbreviation is found on many stamps of the German states and is an abbreviation for the word schilling.

SCHAGIV—This was a unit of value in the Western Ukraine. 100 schagivs were the equivalent of 1 grivna.

SCHILLING—This was a unit of value in which certain stamps of the German Empire were expressed. Usually 16 schillings equaled 1 mark, or 48 schillings equaled 1 thaler.

SCHWAREN—This was a unit of value in the old German state of Oldenburg. 1 schwaren equaled 1/12 of a silbergroschen.

SCINDE DAWK—While the Scinde Dawk stamps are quite rare, the expression is of interest because the word "Scinde" refers to the area controlled by the British East Indies Company, and the word "Dawk" is the Hindu word for post.

SCUDO—This was a unit of value of the Roman states. 1 scudo was worth 100 bajocchi.

SCUTARI DI ALBANIA—This overprint is found on certain stamps of Italy for use at the Italian post office in Scutari, Albania, 1909-16.

S. D.—These initials, meaning "stamp duty," are found overprinted on certain stamps of Hong Kong. They were authorized to be used for postal purposes during a temporary shortage.

S. deN. or S.D.N.—These initials stand for the French expression "Societes de Nations," also known as League of Nations, and are found on the stamps of Switzerland.

SECRET MARKS—Several countries have had secret marks in various issues of stamps. In the U.S.A. the term secret marks usually means the additional markings on the stamps printed by the Continental Bank Note Company in 1873, using the same designs as used by the National Bank Note Co. but distinguished by the markings.

SEEBECK, N.F.—Much has been written about the issues of stamps known as "Seebecks." N. F. Seebeck was the head of the Hamilton Bank Note Co. of N. Y. and in 1899 he made contracts with certain countries of Central America, etc., to print stamps for these governments. He was to supply them with new sets every year, in exchange for which he was to retain the old plates and receive the unsold remainders of the previous sets.

This practice proved to be most unpopular.

SEN—This is a unit of value found on certain stamps of Japan. 1 sen is $\frac{1}{100}$ of 1 yen.

SE-TENANT—This is the French expression meaning "joined together." This usually refers to two stamps of different designs, values, or perforations, etc.; as an unsevered pair.

SEXAGENARY, 1897—This inscription is found on certain stamps of the Leeward Islands, 1897, along with an additional overprint device. The design was in commemoration of the Diamond Jubilee of Queen Victoria.

S. G.—This overprint is found on certain stamps of the Australian state of South Australia prior to 1874 for the official correspondence of the Surveyor-General.

S. G.—These initials perforated or punched into the design of the stamps indicated official postage of the Sudan Government.

SGR—This abbreviation is found in the design of many stamps of the German states and is an abbreviation of the word "silbergroschen."

SHAHI—This was a unit of value found upon certain stamps of Afghanistan and Persia. In Afghanistan the value of 12 shahi were equal to 1 rupee; in Persia, 20 shahi (chahi) were worth 1 kran.

SHAN STATES—The Shan States are in Burma, in both the northern and southern parts of the country. During World War II (1943) the Japanese occupation authorities issued a special set of stamps for use in these states.

SHILLING—The unit of value on stamps of Great Britain and colonies. 20 shillings equal 1 pound sterling.

S. H. S.—These initials are found overprinted on certain stamps of Hungary and mean "Srbska, Hrvatska, Slovenska" or "Serbia, Croatia, Slovenia."

SILBERGROSCHEN—A unit of value of certain stamps of the German states. Usually 30 silbergroschen were equal to 1 thaler.

SILK PAPER, SILK THREAD PAPER— See Dickenson Paper.

SKATIKU—This was a unit of value of the former Lithuanian Republic. 100 skatiku equaled 1 auksinas.

SKILLING—This was a unit of value found on the early stamps of Iceland, Norway, and Denmark.

SKILLING BANCO—This was a unit of value of nineteenth century Sweden. 48 skilling banco equaled 1 riksdaler.

SLD—This abbreviation is for a unit of value found on certain stamps of the Austrian offices in Italy and means "soldi."

S. M.—This overprint is found on certain stamps of the Australian state of South Australia prior to 1874 for the official use of the Stipendary Magistrate.

S. O. 1920—These initials mean "Silesie Orientale" or "Eastern Silesia" and are found on certain stamps of Poland and Czechoslovakia for use in a province of Eastern Silesia.

SOL—This is a unit of value in Peru. 1 sol is worth 100 centavos.

SOLDI—This was a unit of value found on the stamps of Tuscany and the Austrian offices in Italy. 20 soldo were equal to 1 lire; 100 soldi of the Austrian offices in Italy was equal to 1 florin.

SOMERS ISLANDS—This is the former name of the Bermuda Islands.

SONGPY—This was a unit of value in the old kingdom of Siam. 16 songpy were equal to 1 tical.

S. P.—This overprint is found on certain stamps of Luxemburg and means "Service Publique."

S. P. M.—This overprint is found on certain stamps of the French colonial general issue for use in St. Pierre and Miquelon.

SPOORWEGEN—This is the Flemish word for "railroad" and is found on parcel post stamps of Belgium from 1895.

S. T.—This overprint is found on certain stamps of the Australian state of South Australia prior to 1874 for official use of the Superintendent of Telegraphs.

STEINMEYER'S POST—This was a private post organized in 1858 to 1859 in Charleston, West Virginia.

STOTINKI—This is a unit of value in Bulgaria. 100 stotinki equal 1 leva.

STRAIGHT EDGE—This term simply means that a stamp has a straight edge; it should not be confused with a coil stamp or a stamp from a corner of a booklet pane. Straight edge stamps were those stamps from the edges of the sheets of stamps printed by the flat plate process such as the U.S. National Parks etc.; there is a straight edge at the top, or the bottom, or the left or right side of the stamp; then there is a straight edge along the bottom and either right or left side, and along the top and either right or left side. This is due to the sheets having been cut apart rather than separated by perforations.

S. U.—This overprint is found on certain stamps of the Straits Settlements and India, sometimes with a star and crescent. It was for use in the Malay state of Sungei Ujong.

SUCRE—This is a unit of value of Ecuador. 1 centavo equaled 1 sucre.

SURCHARGE—A surcharge is that overprint which changes or alters the face value of a stamp by either increasing the value or reducing the value.

SUSSE PERFORATIONS—This is a private perforation used in France on certain stamps of 1861. A firm of stationers (Susse Bros.) invented a machine to perforate stamps; this they did as a customer service. The holes were very large and they gauged at near 7 per 2 centimeters or 20 millimeters.

SYLLABICS—This expression is usually used when referring to the Katakana numerical alphabet of the Japanese language. In the Japanese issue of 1874 there are secret marks known as syllabics.

SYNCOPATED PERFORATION — This type of peforation was used mainly in the Netherlands some years ago. They used four different types of interruptions or syncopates. They were used mainly in vending machines. The perforation holes were interrupted at various places to somewhat strengthen the delivery of the stamps through the machine.

T

T—This overprint is found on certain stamps of the Australian state of South Australia prior to 1874 for use on official correspondence of the Treasurer.

T—This overprint is found on certain stamps of Abyssinia (Ethiopia) and stands for "postage due."

T—When the letter "T" was perforated into certain stamps of Tasmania, it was indicative of official correspondence.

TAKCA—This inscription is found on postage due stamps of Bulgaria and means "tax."

TAKSE—This overprint is found on certain stamps of Albania and changes them over to postage due stamps.

TALARI—This was a unit of value in Ethiopia equal to 16 mehaleks.

TANGA—This is a unit of value found on certain stamps of Portuguese India. 16 tangas are worth 1 rupia.

TASA—This word is found on the postage due stamps of Uruguay and means "tax."

TAXA DEVIDA—This inscription is found on the postage due stamps of Brazil and means "tax due."

TE BETALEN—This inscription means "to pay" and is found on the postage due stamps of the Netherlands and colonies and Belgium.

TEMESVAR—This free town of Romania was the capital of the Banat Province, It was occupied by the Romanian army during the revolution in Central Europe in 1919, and stamps of Hungary were overprinted for use in this area.

T. E. O.—These initials were applied to certain Turkish stamps for use in Cilicia. The initials mean "Territoires Ennemis Occupe" or "Occupied Enemy Territory."

TETE-BECHE—This is the French term for stamps which have been printed upside down in relation to one another. Stamps printed tete-beche can only be collected in pairs or blocks or larger pieces.

THALER—This was a unit of value in Oldenburg, Hanover, and other states. 30 groschen were the equivalent of 1 thaler.

TICAL—This was a unit of value in the old kingdom of Siam. 64 atts were equivalent to 1 tical. In 1912 the currency was changed and 100 satangs equal 1 tical.

TOMAN—A unit of value in old Persia. Being of gold value, 10 kran equaled 1 toman.

TOPICAL COLLECTING—See page 240.

TORNESE—This was a unit of value found on certain stamps of Neapolitan provinces and Naples. 200 tornese were equal to 1 ducat.

TOTOGI G TOHI—This inscription is found on certain stamps of the island kingdom of Tonga and means "good for postage."

T. R.—This overprint is found on certain stamps of the Australian state of South Australia prior to 1874 for the official use of the Titles Registration Department.

TRANGKA—This was a unit of value in the old kingdom of Tibet. 1 trangka was equal to 6 annas, or 1 sang equaled 6⅔ trangkas.

TRIDENT—A 3 pronged spear of the type usually associated with King Neptune in mythology; applied to stamps of imperial Russia for use in the Ukraine after the revolution of 1917.

TUGHRA—This is the Royal Cypher of the Sultan of Turkey and means "the ever victorious."

U

U. G.—These letters mean "Uganda Government" and are found on the Uganda Protectorate stamps of 1895 which were produced by typewriter.

ULTRAMAR—This word is found on certain stamps of Cuba, etc. and is the Spanish abbreviation for "beyond the sea."

U. P. U.—These letters are the initials of the Universal Postage Union and appear on the stamps of many countries.

UNWATERMARKED—When stamps have been printed on a plain, clear paper, completely free of any design or watermark device, the stamps are referred to as unwatermarked.

UNUSED—A stamp which has not been cancelled and, therefore, still valid for postage.

USED—A stamp that has been used will have a cancellation or defacement mark of some type to indicate it is no longer valid for postage.

USED ABROAD—This term is used to imply stamps of a country used in either colonial offices or regional offices established by the mother country. The area of use can usually be determined from the cancellation, such as the British numeral types.

U. S. P. S.—These letters in either single line or double line form were used in the watermarking of United States stamps between 1895 and 1916; they mean "United States Postage Service."

V

V—This overprint is found on certain stamps of the Australian state of South Australia prior to 1874 for the official correspondence of the Volunteers.

V. A.—This overprint is found on certain stamps of the Australian state of South Australia prior to 1874 for the official correspondence of the Valuator and Auctioneer.

VALE—This overprint is found on certain stamps of the republic of Nicaragua and means "worth."

VAN DIEMAN'S LAND—This was the original name of the British island colony now known as Tasmania, which has since united with Australia.

VARNISH BARS—A pale brown shiny varnish was applied in parallel bars to the face of sheets of certain stamps of Austria from about 1901 to 1905 in an attempt to prevent the public from washing off the cancellations. It did not prove of any value and this practice was discontinued in 1905.

VICHY (ADMINISTRATION)—This name is applied to practically all documents and historical memorabilia which emanated from Vichy in occupied France during World War II. It was at Vichy that Le Marechal Petain tried to maintain a government of France friendly to the occupying German army. None of the governments of the Western world recognized the Vichy Government as being the true republic of the French people; the result being that the many stamps issued from several French colonies were not recognized and even today some are still not recognized as having been issued primarily for postal purposes. The stamps issued in occupied France with the portrait of Petain were used for postal purposes because they were the only stamps available, and the Germans insisted the French use the stamps of Vichy.

VICTORIA LAND—This overprint is found on certain stamps of New Zealand for use of the 1911 South Polar Expedition under the command of Captain Scott. Their base in the Antarctic was to be Victoria Land—therefore, the overprint.

V. N.—This overprint is found on certain stamps of the Australian state of South Australia prior to 1874 for the official use of the Department of Vaccination.

VOOR HET KIND—This Dutch expression means "for the children" and is found on the charity or semi postal stamps of the Netherlands and colonies.

VOORTREKKER— The expression, "The Voortrekker," is of Dutch origin and literally means "one who goes ahead" or "in advance." When one thinks of the Voortrekkers, one usually thinks immediately of South Africa and the Boer War. It was the Voortrekkers, some 8,000 farmers and their families who, being dissatisfied with any and all forms of British government in the Cape Colony, made their now famous trek into the Transvaal in the hinterland of South Africa. Here they set up poorly run and poorly organized bases for a government of themselves. Of the many forms of government established in the Transvaal area, only one was of any strength or had any knowledgeable people within it, and this was the Orange Free State. The Voortrekkers were the people whose descendants, and in some cases the Voortrekkers themselves, engaged in the terror of the Boer War from 1899 through 1902, ending in defeat of the Dutch and the formation of the Union of South Africa.

V. R. I.—These initials mean "Victoria Regina et Imperatrix" or "Victoria, Queen and Empress." They are found as an overprint on certain stamps of the Orange Free State and Transvaal in 1900 during the occupation by British troops in the Boer War.

VUJA-STT-This overprint and inscription is found on the stamps of the Jugoslav district of Trieste. The initials stand for "Vojna Uprava Jugoslovenske Armije, Slobodna Teritorija Trsta," this translates to "Military Administration Jugoslav Army, Free Territory of Trieste."

W

W—This overprint is found on certain stamps of the Australian state of South Australia prior to 1874 for the official correspondence of the Waterworks.

W. A.—These letters, when perforated into the design of certain stamps of the Australian state of Western Australia, indicated they were for official use only.

WATERLOW & SONS LTD.—This is the name of the firm of London stamp printers and engravers who are well known for the beauty of their work.

WATERMARK—During the manufacture of the paper for the production of postage stamps it was the practice to use a design either in single format or in multiples to protect the stamp issued from being flagrantly counterfeited. There are over 350 different watermarks visible to a stamp collector. We refer you to the Whitman book on Worldwide Watermarks and Perforations which gives the reader in a master illustrated book the reference number of all these watermarks of the world.

WATERMARK BITS—See "Bits."

WATERMARK DETECTOR—A watermark detector can be a battery operated viewer or it can be a black glass tray; it must be black in order to properly see the watermark in a stamp. The stamp is placed face down in the tray and a few drops of watermark detector fluid put on the back of the stamp will usually "flash" the watermark into visibility. The new Whitman "WHIT-MARK" watermark tray is made of a new duralin black plastic which is impervious to any and all watermark detection fluids and is unbreakable.

WHARTON'S POST—This was a private post in Louisville, Kentucky, in 1857.

WITWEN UND WAISEN-WOCHE— This overprint is found on certain stamps of Bosnia and means "Widows' and Orphans' Week."

WOVE PAPER—This paper, of smooth and even texture is most generally used in the manufacture of postage stamps.

W. W.—These are the initials of William Wyon, a famous engraver of dies. These initials are visible on certain stamps of Great Britain, 1847-54.

Y

YEN—This is a unit of value in the empire of Japan. 100 sen is equivalent to 1 yen.

YING-YANG—This is the name of a watermark design found in certain stamps of China and, according to celestial philosophy, represent the positive and the negative qualities in nature.

YKP. H. P.—These initials, as an overprint on Austrian stamps, mean "Ukraine Peoples' Republic" and were used during the life of the provisional government in 1918-19, known as Western Ukraine.

Z

Z. A. R.—This overprint is found on certain stamps issued by the Boers for the occupation of the city of Vryburg during the Boer War in 1899; the initials stand for "Zuid Africaansche Republick."

ZEMSTVOS—Even though the Zemstvos are stamps of local nature, they were authorized by the Czar in 1870 when, in order to increase the efficiency of the general postal offices in Russia, the stamps were authorized to be made by the local governments. This has been a very popular field of collecting, and the Zemstvos are not easily found any more today. Some of the Zemstvos are only plain impressions from a hand strike and others are beautifully hand colored.

ADDENDA

The following comparison should be known and remembered by all stamp collectors:

1 BOGUS

2 COUNTERFEIT

Bogus: A fictitious stamp and/or postal marking created to defraud a collector. A bogus stamp and/or postal marking is strictly the creation of a forger. (Often a bogus overprint or surcharge is applied to a genuine stamp. Bogus markings also can be applied to geuine stamps on and/or off cover.)

Counterfeit: An imitation, forgery, of an officially issued postage stamp and/or officially authorized postal marking that has been primarily created to deceive and defraud a collector.

THE PHILATELIC GAZETTEER

Many times we wonder just where a certain country is in our vast world. The following is a reasonably complete list and location of the countries, states, kingdoms, and other political districts from which emanated postage stamps since 1840.

COUNTRY	LOCATION
Abu Dhabi	*Persian Gulf*
Abyssinia (see Ethiopia)	
	Northeastern Africa
Aden	*Southern Arabia*
Aden (Hadhramaut State)	*Eastern Aden*
Aden (Seiyun State)	*Eastern Aden*
Aden (Shihr & Mukalla States)	
	Eastern Aden
Afghanistan	*Central Asia*
Aguera	*Northwest Coast of Africa*
Aitutaki	*South Pacific*
Ajman	*Persian Gulf*
Alaouites	*Western Asia*
Albania	*Southeastern Europe*
Alexandretta (see Hatay)	*Northern Syria*
Algeria	*North Africa*
Allenstein	*East Prussia*
Alsace	*Northern France*
Alwar State	*Northern India*
Anatolia	*Turkey in Asia Minor*
Andorra	*Southern Pyrennees Mountains*
Angola	*Southwestern Africa*
Angra	*Azores Islands*
Anjouan	
	Comoro Islands in Mozambique Channel
Annam and Tonkin	*French Indo China*
Antigua	*West Indies*
Antioquia	*State of Colombia*
Anwhei Province	*East China*
Arabia (Hejaz)	
	Southwestern Asia, Arabian Peninsula
Arabia (Nejd)	
	Southwestern Asia, Arabian Peninsula
Argentina	*South America*
Armenia	*Southern Russia*
Ascension Island	*South Atlantic Ocean*
Australia	*Oceania*
Austria	*Central Europe*
Azerbaijan	*Southern Russia*
Azores Islands	*North Atlantic Ocean*
Baden	*Southwestern Germany*
Bahamas	*West Indies*
Bahawalpur	*Pakistan*
Bahrain	*Persian Gulf*
Bamra State	*Eastern India*
Bangkok	*Siam, Southeast Asia*
Barbados Islands	*West Indies*
Barbuda Island	*West Indies*
Barwani State	*West India*
Basutoland (see Lesotho)	
	Southeastern Africa
Batum	*On the Black Sea, Europe*
Bavaria	*Southern Germany*
Bechuanaland (see Botswana)	
	Central South Africa
Bechuanaland Protectorate	
	Central South Africa
Belgian Congo (see Congo Republic)	
	Central Africa
Belgian East Africa (see Ruanda Urundi)	*Central Africa*
Belgium	*Western Europe*
Benadir (Somalia)	*Eastern Africa*

COUNTRY	LOCATION
Bengasi	*Italian Offices in Africa*
Benin	*West Coast of Africa*
Bergdorf	*Northern Germany*
Bermuda	*West Indies*
Bhopal State	*Central India*
Bhor State	*West India*
Bhutan	*Eastern Himalayas*
Bijawar State	*Central India*
Bohemia-Moravia	*Western Czechoslovakia*
Bolivar	*Colombian State*
Bolivia	*Central South America*
Bosnia-Herzegovina (see Jugoslavia)	*Southern Europe*
Botswana (see Bechuanaland)	
	Central Africa
Boyaca	*Colombian State*
Brazil	
	North and East Coast of South America
Bremen	*Northwestern Germany*
British Antarctic Territory	
	South Atlantic Ocean
British Central Africa	*Central Africa*
British Columbia	
	Northwest Coast of North America
British East Africa	*East Africa*
British Guiana	*Northern South America*
British Honduras	*Central America*
British Solomon Islands	
	West Pacific Ocean
British Somaliland	*Eastern Africa*
Brunei	*Northwest Coast of Borneo*
Brunswick	*Northern Germany*
Bulgaria	*Southeastern Europe*
Bundi State	*Northwest India*
Burma	*Northern India*
Burundi	*Central Africa*
Bushire	*On the Persian Gulf*
Bussahir State	*North India*
Cabo Gracias a Dios	*Northeast Nicaragua*
Cabo (Cape) Juby	
	Northwest Coast of Africa
Cabo (Cape) Verde Islands	
	Atlantic Ocean off Southwest Coast of Africa
Calchi, Aegean Island	*Aegean Sea*
Calino, Aegean Island	*Aegean Sea*
Cambodia	*Southeast Asia*
Cameroon	*West Coast of Africa*
Canada Dominion	*North America*
Canal Zone	*Central America*
Canary Islands	
	Atlantic Ocean, off North Africa
Cape of Good Hope	
	Southern Part of South America
Carchi, Aegean Island	*Aegean Sea*
Carinthia	*Southern Europe*
Caroline Island	*West Pacific Ocean*
Carpatho-Ukraine	*Central Europe*
Caso, Aegean Island	*Aegean Sea*
Castellorizo	*Mediterranean Sea*
Cauca	*Colombian State*
Cavalla (Greek Offices)	*Offices in Turkey*
Cavalle (French Offices)	*Offices in Turkey*

COUNTRY	LOCATION

Cayman Islands.............*West Indies*
Celebes Islands (Japanese Occup.)...
   South Pacific Ocean, Celebes, Banda and Java Seas
Central African Republic..*Western Africa*
Central Lithuania....*Northeastern Europe*
Ceylon.....................*Indian Ocean*
Chad.....................*Central Africa*
Chamba State........*North Central India*
Charkhari State.....*North Central India*
Chekiang Province...........*East China*
Chile.....................
   Southwestern Coast of South America
China....................*Eastern Asia*
Chios, Aegean Island (Greek)..*Aegean Sea*
Christmas Island............*Indian Ocean*
Cilicia.........*Southeastern Asia Minor*
Cochin....................*South India*
Cocos and Keeling Islands...*Indian Ocean*
Colombia...........................
   Northwestern Coast of South America
Comoro Island.....*Mozambique Channel*
Confederate States..*Southern United States*
Congo Republic....................
   (See Belgian Congo, Central Africa, French Middle Congo, Western Africa)
Coo, Aegean Island (Italian)..*Aegean Sea*
Cook Island.........*South Pacific Ocean*
Corfu (Greek)...............*Ionian Sea*
Costa Rica..............*Central America*
Council of Europe................
   Strasbourg, Luxembourg
Crete...............*Mediterranean Sea*
Croatia.............*Southeastern Europe*
Croatia-Slovenia (Jugoslavia)........
   Southern Europe
Cuba.....................*West Indies*
Curacao (Netherlands Antiles)..........
   West Indies
Cyprus...............*Mediterranean Sea*
Cyrenaica..................*North Africa*
Czechoslovakia...........*Central Europe*

Dahomey..........*West Coast of Africa*
Dalmatia (Italian Occupation).......
   Northwest Part of the Balkan Peninsula
Danish West Indies ....*West Indies*
Danzig.................*Northern Europe*
Debrecen................*Central Europe*
Dedeagatch (Greek)..............*Turkey*
Dedeagh (French................*Turkey*
   Foreign Offices in Turkey
Denmark...........*Northwestern Europe*
Dhar State...........*West Central India*
Diego Suarez......................
   Northern Part of Madagascar Island
Djibouti.................*Eastern Africa*
Dominica...................*West Indies*
Dominican Republic.........*West Indies*
Dubai.....................*Persian Gulf*
Durazzo (Italian Office).........*Turkey*
Dutch East Indies...........*East Indies*
Dutch New Guinea.................
   Southwest Pacific Ocean
Duttia State........*North Central India*

Egypt..................*Northern Africa*
Elobey, Annobon and Corisca
(Spanish)...*Offshore Islands near Guinea, Western Africa*
Epirus (Greek)......*Southeastern Europe*
Eritrea.................*Northeast Africa*
Estonia.................*Northern Europe*

COUNTRY	LOCATION

Ethiopia (Abbyssinia)...*Northeast Africa*
Eupen.................*Northern Belgium*

Falkland Islands.....*East of the Southern Tip of South America*
Falkland Island Dependencies........
   East of the Southern Tip of South America
Far Eastern Republic............*Siberia*
Faridkot State........*North Central India*
Federated Malay States.............
   Malay Peninula. Comprised of the states of Negri-Sembliam, Perak, Pahang, Selangor.
Federation of Malaya..............
   Comprised of the states of Kedeh, Kalantan, Johore, Negri-Sembliam, Pahang, Perlis, Perak, Trengganu and Malacca and Penang settlements.
Fernando Po.............*Gulf of Guinea*
Fezzan Ghadames (French Occupied Libia)................*Northern Africa*
Fiji Islands..........*South Pacific Ocean*
Finland................*Northern Europe*
Fiume................*On the Adriatic Sea*
Foochow.....*Seaport in Southeast China*
Formosa (Nationalist Republic of China)......................
   Island of Taiwan, East of the China Coast.
France...................*Western Europe*
French Congo ....*Central Africa*
French Equatorial Africa...........
   North Central Africa
French Guiana ....*South America*
French Guinea.......*West African Coast*
French India..........*East Coast of India*
French Oceania (Polynesia)..........
   South Pacific Ocean
French Southern and Antarctic Territ.....................*Antarctica*
French Sudan..........*Northwest Africa*
French West Africa.....*Northwest Africa*
Fujeira....................*Gulf of Oman*
Funchal..........................
   In the Madeira Is. Northwest of Africa

Gabon..............*West Coast of Africa*
Galapagos Islands (Ecuador)........
   Offshore Islands West of Ecuador in South America
Gambia............*West Coast of Africa*
Georgia.....*Southern Part of Russia*
German East Africa........*East Africa*
German New Guinea...*West Pacific Ocean*
German Southwest Africa............
   Southwest Africa
Germany...............*Northern Europe*
Ghana (see Gold Coast)..............
   West Coast of Africa
Gibraltar..............*Mediterranean Sea*
Gilbert and Ellice Island...........
   South Pacific Ocean
Gold Coast (see Ghana).....*West Africa*
Graham Land (Falkland Dep.)......
   East of the Southern Tip of South America
Great Britain.....................
   West of European Continent
Greece..............*Southeastern Europe*
Greenland..........*North Atlantic Ocean*
Grenada ....*West Indies*
Griqualand West...........*South Africa*

COUNTRY	LOCATION
Guadaloupe	West Indies
Guam	Philippine Sea
Guanacaste (Costa Rica)	
	Northwest Coast of Central America
Guatemala	Central America
Guinea Republic	West Africa Coast
Guyana Republic (see British Guiana)	
	Northeast Coast of South America
Gwalior State	North Central India
Haiti	West Indies
Hamburg	Northern Germany
Hanover	Northern Germany
Hatay (Alexandretta)	
	Northwest Coast of Africa
Hawaii	Pacific Ocean
Heligoland	Offshore Island
	Near the North Coast of Germany
Holkar (Indore State)	West Central India
Honan Province	Eastern China
Honduras	Central America
Hong Kong	An Island and
	Peninsula in Southeast China
Hopei Province	Northeastern China
Horta	In the Azores Islands
Hunan Province	Eastern China
Hungary	Central Europe
Hupeh Province	East Central China
Hyderabad State	Central India
Icaria (Greek Aegean Island)	
	Aegean Sea
Iceland	North Atlantic Ocean
Idar State	West Africa
Ifni	North Africa
India	South Central Asia
Indo-China (French)	Southeastern Asia
Indonesia	East Indies
Indore State	West Central Africa
	(see Holkar)
Inhambane	East Africa
Inini	Northeastern South America
Inner Mongolia	Northern China
International Court of Justice	
(Netherlands)	The Hague, Netherlands
Ionian Islands (British)	
	Mediterranean Sea
Iran (Persia)	Western Asia
Iraq (British Mandate)	Western Asia
Ireland	North Atlantic Ocean
Israel	Western Asia
Istria (Jugoslavia)	Southern Europe
Italian East Africa	East Africa
Italian Somaliland (see Somalia)	
	East Africa
Italy	Southern Europe
Ivory Coast (French)	
	West Coast of Africa
Ivory Coast Republic	
	West Coast of Africa
Jaipur State	North Central India
Jamaica	West Indies
Jammu and Kashmir State	
	Northern India
Japan	North Pacific Ocean
Jasdan State	Western India
Jeend State (also Jhind)	
	Northern Punjab Area, North India
Jhind State (also Jeend)	
	Northern Punjab Area, North India
Johore State (Malaya)	
	Southern Malay Peninsula

COUNTRY	LOCATION
Jordan	Near East
Juan Fernandez Islands (Chile)	
	West of Valparaiso, Chile
Jugoslavia	Southern Europe
Kansu Province	North Central China
Karelia	Northwestern Soviet Russia
Karki (Italy Aegean Island)	Aegean Sea
Kashmir State	Northern India
Kedah State (Malaya)	
	West Coast, Malay Peninsula
Kelantan State (Malaya)	
	East Coast, Malay Peninsula
Kenya Republic	East Africa
Kenya, Uganda Tanganyika	East Africa
Khor Fakkan (Sharjah Dependency)	
	Gulf of Oman
Kiangsi Province	Northeast China
Kiatchau (German Colony, China)	
	Shantung Peninsula, China
Kionga	Southeast Africa
Kishangarh State	Northwest India
Korea	Peninsula Between the Sea
	of Japan and the Yellow Sea
Kuwait	In the Persian Gulf
Kwangsi Province	Southeast China
Kwangtung Province	Southeast China
Kweichow Province	Southeast China
Labuan	East Indies
Lagos	West Africa
Laos	Southeast Asia
Las Bela State	Northwest India
Latakia (Alaouites)	Western Asia
Latvia	Northern Europe
Lebanon	Asia Minor
Leeward Islands	East Indies
Lemnos (Greek Aegean Island)	
	Aegean Sea
Lero (Italian Aegean Island)	
	Aegean Sea
Lesbos (Mytilene) (Greek Aegean Is.)	
	Aegean Sea
Lesotho (Basutoland)	
	Southwestern Africa
Liberia	West Coast of Africa
Libia	North Africa
Liechtenstein	Central Europe
Lipso (Italy Aegean Island)	Aegean Sea
Lisso	Aegean Sea
Lithuania	Northern Europe
Lombardy-Venetia (Austrian Italy)	
	Northern Italy
Lorraine	Northern France
Lourenco Marques	Southeast Africa
Lubeck	On the Baltic Sea
Ljubljana (Jugoslavia)	Southern Europe
Luxembourg	Western Europe
Macao	At the Mouth
	of the Canton River, China Coast
Madagascar (Malagasy Republic)	
	Island Off the Coast of Southeastern
	Africa
Madeira	Northwest of Africa,
	Atlantic Ocean
Mafeking	South Africa
Magdalena	State of Colombia,
	South America
Malacca	Southern Malay Peninsula,
	Southwest Asia
Malawi State (Br. Nyasaland)	
	Southern Africa
Malaysia	Northwestern Borneo and
	Malay Peninsula

— 200 —

COUNTRY	LOCATION
Maldive Islands	Indian Ocean
Mali	West Africa
Malmedy	Northern Belgium
Malta	Mediterranean Sea
Manchukuo	Northeastern China
Manchuria Province	Northeastern China
Mariana Islands	West Pacific Ocean
Marienwerder	Northeastern Germany
Marshall Islands (German Colony)	West Pacific Ocean
Martinique	West Indies
Mauritania	Northwest Africa
Mauritius	Indian Ocean
Mayotte	Mozambique Channel
Mecklenburg-Schwerin	Northern Germany
Mecklenburg-Strelitz	Northern Germany
Memel	Northern Europe
Mesopotamia (Br. Occupation)	Western Africa
Mexico	Central America
Middle Congo (Republic of the Congo)	Western Africa
Modena	Northern Italy
Moheli	Mozambique Channel
Moldavia-Wallachia	Southeastern Europe
Monaco	Southern Europe
Mongolia	Central Asia
Montenegro	Southern Europe
Montserrat	West Indies
Morocco	Northwest Coast of Africa
Morvi State	Western India
Mozambique	Southeast Africa
Muscat-Oman	Southeastern Part of the Arabian Peninsula
Nabha State	Northern India
Naples	Southern Italy
Natal	South Africa
Nauru	West Central Pacific Ocean
Negri-Sembilan State	West Coast, Malay Peninsula
Nepal	Himalaya Mountains, Southwest Central Asia
Netherlands	Northwestern Europe
Netherlands Antilles (Curacao)	West Indies
Nevis	West Indies
New Britain (British Occup. German New Guinea	South Pacific Ocean
New Brunswick	Eastern Canada
New Caledonia	South Pacific Ocean
Newfoundland	In the Atlantic Ocean Off the Coast of Northeastern Canada
New Greece (Greek Occup. Turkey)	Southeastern Europe
New Guinea	South Pacific Ocean
New Hebrides	South Pacific Ocean
New Republic	South Africa
New South Wales	Southeast Coast of Australia
New Zealand	South Pacific Ocean
Nicaragua	Central America
Niger Republic	Northern Africa
Niger Coast	West Coast of Africa
Nigeria	West Coast of Africa
Niue	South Pacific Ocean
Norfolk Island	South Pacific Ocean
North Borneo	Northern Part of the Island of Borneo
North China	North China
North Epirus (Greek Occ. Albania)	Southeastern Europe

COUNTRY	LOCATION
North German Confederation	Northern Germany
North Ingermanland	Northern Russia
North West Pacific Islands	West Pacific Ocean
Nossi Be	Indian Ocean Off of Madagascar
Nova Scotia	West Coast of Canada
Nowanugger State	Western India
Nyasaland Protectorate (see Malawi)	Southern Africa
Nyassa	Southeast Africa
Obock	Eastern Africa, Seaport on the Gulf of Aden
Oil Rivers Protectorate	West Coast of Africa on the Gulf of Guinea
Oldenburg	Northwest Germany
Oltre Giuba (Jubaland)	East Africa
Orange River Colony (Orange Free State)	South Africa
Orcha State	Central India
Pahang State (Malaya)	East Coast, Malay Peninsula
Pakistan	South Central Asia
Palestine	Western Asia
Panama	Central America
Papua-New Guinea	South Pacific, North of Australia
Paraguay	South America
Parma	Northern Italy
Patiala State	Northern India
Patmo (Aegean Island)	Aegean Sea
Penang State (Malaya)	West Coast of the Malay Peninsula
Penrhyn Island	South Pacific Ocean
Perak State (Malaya)	West Coast of the Malay Peninsula
Perlis State (Malaya)	West Coast of the Malay Peninsula
Persia (Iran)	Western Asia
Peru	South America
Philippine Islands	North Pacific Ocean
Piscopi (Aegean Island)	Aegean Sea
Pitcairn Island	South Pacific
Poland	Central Europe
Ponta Delgada	Azores Islands
Poonch State	Northern India
Port Lagos	Turkey
Portugal	Southern Europe
Portuguese Congo	Southwest Coast of Africa
Portuguese Guinea	West Coast of Africa
Portuguese India	West Coast of India
Prince Edward Island	In the Gulf of St. Lawrence
Prussia	Northern Germany
Puerto Rico	West Indies
Puttialla State (see Patialia State)	
Qatar	Eastern Arabia
Queensland	Northeastern Australia
Quelimane	East Africa
Rajasthan State	Northwest India
Rajpeepla State	West India
Rarotonga	South Pacific Ocean
Ras al Khaima	Persian Gulf
Reunion Island	Indian Ocean
Rheinland Pfalz	Southern Germany, Palatinate Area
Rhodes (Aegean Island)	Aegean Sea

COUNTRY	LOCATION

Rhodesia.............*Southeastern Africa*
Rio de Oro......*Northwest Coast of Africa*
Rio Muni.................*West Africa*
Romagna..............*Southern Italy*
Romania...........*Southeastern Europe*
Ross Dependency...........*South Pacific*
Rouad Island.........*Mediterranean Sea*
Ruanda-Urundi (Belgian Congo).....
Central Africa
Russia..*Eastern Europe and Northern Asia*
Rwanda................*Central Africa*
Ryukyu Islands...........*East China Sea*

Saar..................*Western Europe*
Sabah...............*Northeastern Borneo*
St. Christopher..............*West Indies*
St. Christopher, Nevis, Anguilla......
West Indies
St. Helena..*Atlantic Ocean, West of Africa*
St. Lucia....................*West Indies*
St. Marie de Madagascar Island....
Off East Madagascar
St. Pierre et Miquelon Islands.......
Off the Southern Coast of Newfoundland,
Northeast Canada
St. Thomas and Prince Isalnds.......
In the Gulf of Guinea, West Coast of
Africa
St. Vincent Island..........*West Indies*
Salvador...............*Central America*
Samoa...............*South Pacific Ocean*
Samos Island................*Aegean Sea*
San Marino................*Eastern Italy*
Santander...........*A State of Colombia,*
South America
Sarawak...............*Northwest Borneo*
Sardinia Island.......*Mediterranean Sea*
Saseno Island..............*Adriatic Sea*
Saudi Arabia.........*Southwestern Asia,*
Arabian Peninsula
Saxony.................*Central Germany*
Schleswig.............*Northern Germany*
Schleswig-Holstein....*Northern Germany,*
and Part of the Jutland Peninsula
Selangor State (Malaya)........
West Coast of the Malay Peninsula
Senegal.............*West Coast of Africa*
Serbia...............*Southeastern Europe*
Seychelles Islands...........*Indian Ocean*
Shanghai........*Whangpoo River, China*
Shansi Province........*Northeast China*
Shantung Province.......*Northeast China*
Sharjah.....................*Persian Gulf*
Siam (Thailand)...........*Southeast Asia*
Siberia...................*Northern Asia*
Sicily, Island of......*Mediterranean Sea*
Sierra Leone........*West Coast of Africa*
Simi (Aegean Island).........*Aegean Sea*
Singapore Island........*Off the Southern*
Part of the Malay Peninsula
Sinkiang Province........*Northwest China*
Sirmoor State................*North India*
Slovakia...................*Central Europe*
Slovenia (Jugoslavia)....*Southern Europe*
Somali Coast..............*Eastern Africa*
Somalia..................*Eastern Africa*
Somaliland Protectorate...*Eastern Africa*
Soruth State (see Saurashtra)....
Western India
South Africa...........*Southern Africa*
South Arabia Federation..*Southern Arabia*
South Australia....*Central South Australia*
South Bulgaria (Eastern Rumelia)....
Southern Bulgaria, Southeastern Europe

COUNTRY	LOCATION

South Georgia (Falkland Dependency)
.................*South Atlantic Ocean*
South Orkneys (Falkland Dependency)
.................*South Atlantic Ocean*
South Russia...........*Southern Russia,*
on the Black and Caspian Seas
South Shetlands (Falkland Dependency)
.................*South Atlantic Ocean*
South Viet Nam......*Southeastern Asia*
South West Africa.................
Southwestern Part of Africa
Southern Cameroons..*West Coast of Africa*
Southern Nigeria.........*Western Africa*
Southern Rhodesia....*Southwestern Africa*
Spain...............*Southwestern Europe*
Spanish Guinea..........*Western Africa*
Spanish Morocco.......*Northwest Africa*
Spanish Sahara........*Northwest Africa*
Spanish West Africa.....*Northwest Africa*
Stampalia (Aegean Island)....*Aegean Sea*
Stellaland..................*South Africa*
Straits Settlements.....*Southeastern Asia,*
Malay Peninsula
Sudan...............*Northeastern Africa*
Sungei-Ujong (Malay State).........
West Malay Coast
Supeh Province.........*Northwest China*
Surinam...........................
Northeast Coast of South America
Swaziland...................*South Africa*
Sweden.................*Northern Europe*
Switzerland...............*Central Europe*
Syria (French Mandate).....*Western Asia*
Szechwan Province.........*Central China*

Tahiti Island.........*South Pacific Ocean*
Tanganyika...........*Southeastern Africa*
Tangier..................*Northern Africa*
Tannu Tuva......*Northwestern Mongolia*
Tanzania.............*Southwestern Africa*
Tasmania Island...................
Off the Southeast Coast of Australia
Tete.................*Southeastern Africa*
Tetuan........*Northwest Coast of Africa*
Thessaly............*Southeastern Europe*
Thrace.............*Southeastern Europe*
Thurn and Taxis........*Western Germany*
Tibet......................*Central Asia*
Timor.............*South Pacific Ocean,*
Part of Malay Archipelago
Tobago................... *West India*
Togo.....................*Western Africa*
Tokelau Island.......*South Pacific Ocean*
Tolima................*State of Colombia,*
South America
Trans-Jordan.................*Near East*
Transcaucasian Federated Republics ....
Southeastern Europe
Transvaal....................*South Africa*
Travancore State............*South India*
Trengannu......*Eastern Malay Peninsula*
Trieste..............*On the Adriatic Sea*
Trinidad....................*West Indies*
Trinidad and Tobago........*West Indies*
Tripoli (Italy Offices, Africa)........
Northern Africa
Tripolitania..............*Northern Africa*
Tristan da Cunha...*South Atlantic Ocean*
Trucial States...............*Persian Gulf*
Tunisia.....................*North Africa*
Turkey.............*Southeastern Europe,*
Western Asia
Turks Islands.................*West Indies*
Turks and Caicos Islands.....*West Indies*

COUNTRY	LOCATION
Tuscany.............*North Central Italy*	
Two Sicilies, Neopolitan Province....	
	Southern Italy
Ubangi (French Colony)...*Western Africa*	
Uganda Protectorate..........*East Africa*	
Ukraine................*Southwest Russia*	
Umm al Qiwain.............*Persian Gulf*	
United Arab Republic.....*Northern Africa*	
United Nations...*New York City, U.S.A.*	
United States.............*North America*	
Upper Senegal and Niger............	
	Northwest Africa
Upper Silesia...........*Eastern Germany*	
Upper Volta............*Northwest Africa*	
Uruguay.................*South America*	
Vancouver Island..................	
	Northwest Coast of North America
Van Diemensland (Tasmania).......	
	Off the Southeast Coast of Australia
Vathy (French Offices, Turkey)...*Turkey*	
Vatican City..............*Western Italy*	
Venezia Guilia......*South Central Europe*	

COUNTRY	LOCATION
Venezuela.................*South America*	
Victoria..........*Southeastern Australia*	
Virgin Islands...............*West Indies*	
Wadhwan State..............*West India*	
Walachia...........*Southeastern Europe*	
Wallis et Futuna......*South Pacific Ocean*	
Western Australia..................	
	Western Part of Australia
Western Samoa......*South Pacific Ocean*	
Western Ukraine.....*East Central Europe*	
West Irian (West New Guinea).......	
	South Pacific Ocean
West New Guinea.....*South Pacific Ocean*	
Wurttemberg..........*Southern Germany*	
Yemen.................*Southern Arabia*	
Yunnan Province....*South Central China*	
Zambezia....................*East Africa*	
Zanzibar Islands...................	
	Off the Coast of East Africa
Zululand....................*South Africa*	

SPANISH CIVIL WAR
JULY 17, 1936 TO MARCH 29, 1939

In order that the various issues from each government as well as the provinces and towns in the same government may be properly understood and classified, it is necessary to remember the different names of the Republican and Nationalist governments. The various names given each side are:

Republican Government:

Republic; Republican Government; Government; Republicans; Government Forces; Loyalist Government; Madrid Government; Valencia Government; People's Front; Legitimate Government of Spain; Communist Government; Marxists; Reds.

Nationalist Government:

Franco Government; Franco Forces; Nationalist Government; Insurgents; Insurgent Government; Burgos Government; Gen. Franco's Domain; Spanish Nationalist Government; Liberated Parts of Spain; Fascist Government; Landlord's Government; Church's Government; Rebels.

Usually the stamp or issue can be identified by the definitive inscription used by each government or province. "CORREO" and "CORREOS" are used by both sides, and "CORREUS" is found only on those stamps from the province of Catalonia which was affiliated with the Loyalist Government.

"REPUBLICA ESPONOLA" is usually found on the stamps issued by the Loyalists, except on the provisional or municipal issues from Catalonia where "REPUBLICA ESPANYOLA" is used.

"ARRIBA ESPANA!" and "VIVA FRANCO" are found only on the stamps or labels issued by the Franco forces.

"ESPANA" although occasionally seen on Loyalist issues is always used instead of "ESPANOLA" on the regular issues of the Nationalist Government. The Spanish words "Communicaciones," "Catalonia" and "Ayuntamiento," when used on stamps or sheets issued in Catalonia are written "Communicacions," "Catalunya" and "Ajuntament."

The following are a few of the more important inscriptions, with their proper English translation, used on the various Civil War Issues:

Arriba Espana!, Arise Spain (Slogan of Fascist in Spain); Viva Franco, Long Life Franco; II Ano Triumfal, Second Year of Triumph; Assistencia Social, Social Aid, or, Public Welfare; Beneficencia, Charity; Pro La Patria, For the Fatherland; Saludo a Franco, Salute, or Greetings to Franco; Alzamiento Nacional, Nationalist Uprising; Falange Espanola, Spanish Phalanx or Group (Sp. Fascist Party); Ayuntamiento de, Municipal Government of, or, Town Hall of; Diputacion Provincial, Provincial Council; Junta Tecnica del Estado, Technical Council of State; Gaudillo de Espana, Leader of Spain; Marruecos, Morocco; Para Obrero, Unemployed Workmen; Cocinas Economicas, Municipal Kitchens.

MAPS OF STAMP ISSUING AREAS

Maps have always held a fascination for man because the map or outline gives a direction or tells of a location. Maps are also important to stamp collectors as a vital part of knowing his or her stamps.

The world today is seeing many new countries emerge into the light of freedom, independence and self determination. These new nations are so well documented and written up in the daily press that almost every collector has a reasonably good background of information about their geography.

But what of the countries and provinces which are no longer sovereign even though stamps do exist as issued and as cancelled by the governments of these countries or provinces while they were sovereign areas?

The following pages depict some of the areas which all of us know in a general way, but when one looks at a map of the Feudatory States of India and realizes the proximity of one state to another, or the size of the states of the old German Empire, one stands in awe of the ability of a little postage stamp to perform its duty.

It would not be possible to show maps of every stamp issuing area in this book, but there are a few areas which are interesting, exciting and some almost mysterious in their location in the world.

Islands of the Aegean Islands Group

ISLANDS OF THE
AEGEAN ISLANDS GROUP

1. Calchi
2. Calino
3. Caso
4. Coo (Kos, Cos)
5. Lero
6. Lisso
7. Nisiro
8. Patmo
9. Piscopi
10. Rhodes
11. Simi
12. Stampalia

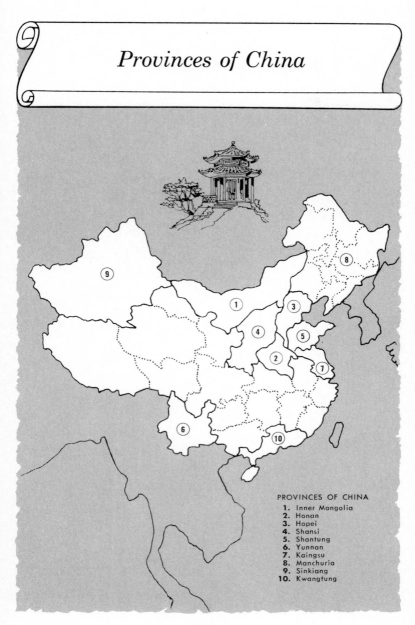

Provinces of China

PROVINCES OF CHINA
1. Inner Mongolia
2. Honan
3. Hopei
4. Shansi
5. Shantung
6. Yunnan
7. Kaingsu
8. Manchuria
9. Sinkiang
10. Kwangtung

States of the Republic of Colombia

STATES OF COLOMBIA
1. Antioquia
2. Bolivar
3. City of Medellín
4. Boyaca
5. Cauca
6. Cundinamarca
7. Magdalena
8. Santander
9. Tolima

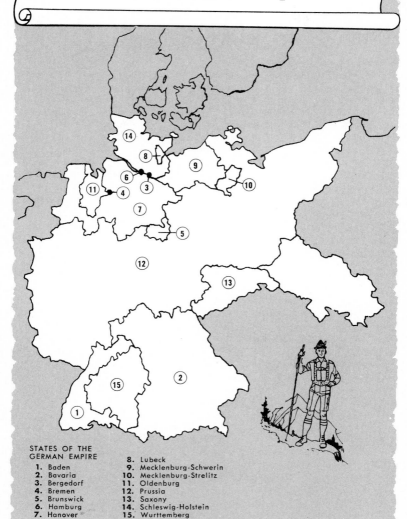

States of the German Empire
Continental Europe

STATES OF THE
GERMAN EMPIRE
1. Baden
2. Bavaria
3. Bergedorf
4. Bremen
5. Brunswick
6. Hamburg
7. Hanover
8. Lubeck
9. Mecklenburg-Schwerin
10. Mecklenburg-Strelitz
11. Oldenburg
12. Prussia
13. Saxony
14. Schleswig-Holstein
15. Wurttemberg

States of the
Kingdom of Italy

STATES OF THE
KINGDOM OF ITALY

1. Modena
2. Parma
3. Romagna
4. Sardinia
5. Tuscany
6. Naples
7. Sicily

Islands of the West Indies

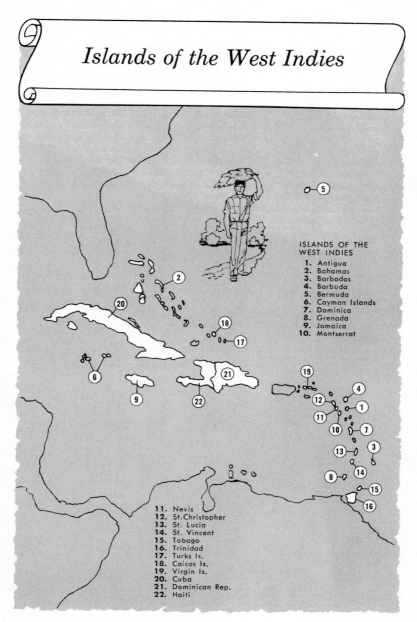

ISLANDS OF THE WEST INDIES

1. Antigua
2. Bahamas
3. Barbados
4. Barbuda
5. Bermuda
6. Cayman Islands
7. Dominica
8. Grenada
9. Jamaica
10. Montserrat
11. Nevis
12. St. Christopher
13. St. Lucia
14. St. Vincent
15. Tobago
16. Trinidad
17. Turks Is.
18. Caicos Is.
19. Virgin Is.
20. Cuba
21. Dominican Rep.
22. Haiti

States of the Malay Peninsula

STATES OF THE MALAY

1. Johore
2. Kedah
3. Kelantan
4. Malacca
5. Negri Sembilan
6. Pahang
7. Penang
8. Perak
9. Perlis
10. Selangor
11. Sungei Ujong
12. Trengganu

Countries of the
Persian Gulf Area

COUNTRIES OF THE
PERSIAN GULF AREA
1. Abu Dhabi
2. Aden
3. Ajman
4. Bahrain
5. Dubai
6. Fujeira
7. Muscat-Oman
8. Qatar
9. Ras al Khaima
10. Sharjah
11. South Arabia
12. Trucial States
13. Umm al Qiwain

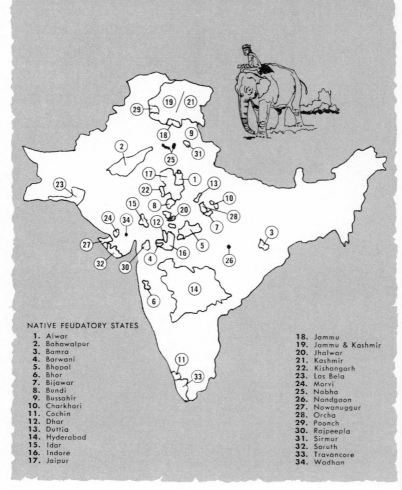

Native Feudatory States of India

NATIVE FEUDATORY STATES
1. Alwar
2. Bahawalpur
3. Bamra
4. Barwani
5. Bhopal
6. Bhor
7. Bijawar
8. Bundi
9. Bussahir
10. Charkhari
11. Cochin
12. Dhar
13. Duttia
14. Hyderabad
15. Idar
16. Indore
17. Jaipur
18. Jammu
19. Jammu & Kashmir
20. Jhalwar
21. Kashmir
22. Kishangarh
23. Las Bela
24. Morvi
25. Nabha
26. Nandgaon
27. Nowanuggur
28. Orcha
29. Poonch
30. Rajpeepla
31. Sirmur
32. Soruth
33. Travancore
34. Wadhan

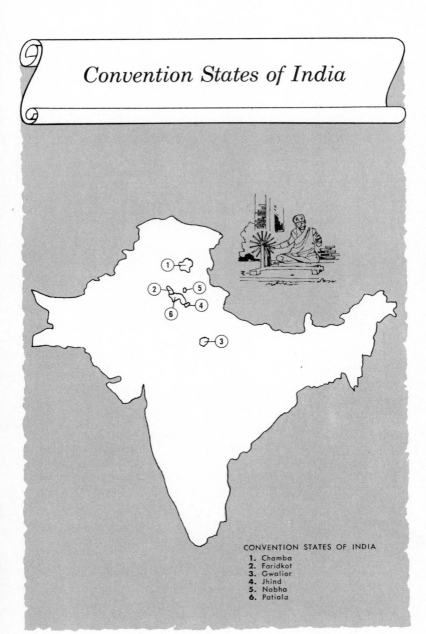

Convention States of India

CONVENTION STATES OF INDIA
1. Chamba
2. Faridkot
3. Gwalior
4. Jhind
5. Nabha
6. Patiala

Lithographic Process (OFFSET PRINTING)

PRINCIPLE OF LITHOGRAPHY...

RULE: GREASE AND WATER REPEL EACH OTHER

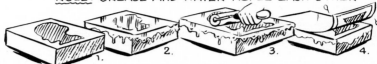

1. GREASE-PENCIL OR INK DESIGN IS DRAWN ON FINE GROUND STONE. 2. SURFACE OF STONE IS WATERED. 3. INK IS ROLLED ON SURFACE – GREASE DRAWING TAKES INK – REST OF STONE (WATERED) REPELS INK. 4. DAMPENED PAPER IS ROLLED ON WET STONE, PRINTING ONLY THE INKED DRAWING.

SAME PRINCIPLE APPLIES TO OFFSET PRINTING. THE PHOTO-MECHANICAL DESIGN IS ETCHED (ACID) ON THE SURFACE OF PLATE. IMAGE IS FIXED ON PLATE BY CHEMICALS, AND PRINTING IS DONE ON A LITHO-PRESS.

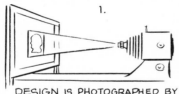

1. DESIGN IS PHOTOGRAPHED BY REPRODUCTION CAMERA...

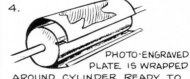

4. PHOTO-ENGRAVED PLATE IS WRAPPED AROUND CYLINDER READY TO TRANSFER IMAGE TO RUBBER PRINTING BLANKET...

2. FILM NEG. ARC LIGHT — SENSITIZED METAL PLATE
BRILLIANT LIGHT TRANSFERS IMAGE FROM NEGATIVE TO PLATE...

5. PLATE RUBBER BLANKET PAPER

3. EMULSION IS WIPED ON, 'FIXING' IMAGE TO PLATE...

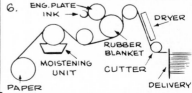

6. ENG. PLATE INK DRYER RUBBER BLANKET MOISTENING UNIT CUTTER DELIVERY PAPER

ON ROTOGRAVURE PROCESS, NO WATER IS USED – VARIOUS THICKNESSES OF APPLIED INK ON PAPER DETERMINES (BY ROUGH FEEL) GRAVURE.

Printing of Stamps

1.

ARTIST'S
LAYOUT SKETCH

2.

ENGRAVER
CUTTING IN SOFT STEEL DIE

3.

HARDENED DIE
IS ROLLED OVER
SOFT STEEL PLATE
TO TRANSFER
DESIGN

4.

A SERIES OF TRANSFERS
MADE FROM ENGRAVED DIE

5.

INK IS ROLLED ON PLATE
FILLING EVERY ENGRAVED
CUT WITH INK ...

6.

PLATE IS WIPED CLEAN
AND THEN BURNISHED ...

7. END VIEW

PLATE WITH INK-FILLED
ENGRAVING READY FOR
PRESS ...

8.

BY PRESSURE OF
PRINTING ROLLER, THE
INK-FILLED CUTS ARE
'SQUEEZED' ONTO DAMP
FIBEROUS PAPER, GIVING CLEAR
IMAGE OF ENGRAVED DESIGN...

9.

PRINTED SHEETS ARE DRIED
AND PRESSED FLAT READY
FOR PERFORATING.

Gumming of Stamps

HERE, ROWLAND, I FOUND THIS STAMP STICK-ING TO YOUR SLEEVE~!

SIR ROWLAND HILL, IN 1837, WAS SAID TO HAVE BEEN THE FIRST MAN TO MAKE AN ADHESIVE STAMP.

IN THE EARLY DAYS, PRINTERS ADDED SOME KIND OF LIQUID ADHESIVE BY BRUSH, RAGS, OR DAUBER, THEN HUNG THEM TO DRY. ONCE DRY, THEY WOULD ROLL THEM FIRST ONE WAY, THEN THE OTHER TO 'BREAK' THE GUM TO PREVENT CURLING. NOW STAMP GUM IS USUALLY WHITE, NON-CURLING, AND NON-CRACKING. INGREDIENTS USED ARE: VEG-ETABLE MATTER, DEXTROSE, MOLASSES, ETC., AND

"...WASHING? — NO, IT'S OUR NUTTY NEIGHBOR HANGING OUT HIS STAMP PAPER!!"

ARE SAFE TO USE AS ADHESIVE.
GUMMING IS ALSO IMPORTANT
IN DETECTION OF STAMP FOR-
GERIES, AND MAKES IT DIFFICULT
TO MATCH CONTENT, COLOR,
AGE, ETC.

ORIGINAL GUM

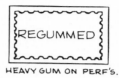

HEAVY GUM ON PERF'S.

SOME STAMPS FROM DIFFERENT COUNTRIES ARE
UNGUMMED DUE TO LACK OF FACILITIES AND
CLIMATIC CONDITIONS. THESE STAMPS ARE
STILL CONSIDERED AS MINT STAMPS EVEN
THOUGH THEY WERE ISSUED WITHOUT GUM.

REGUMMING IS DONE WHEN STAMPS HAVE
LOST THEIR ORIGINAL ADHESIVE. TO AVOID
THE COLLECTOR'S SUSPICION, THESE SHOULD
BE MARKED "REGUMMED" ON THE BACK.

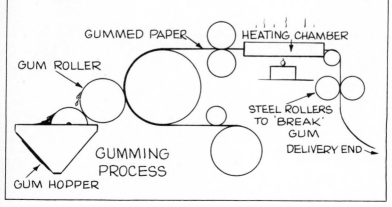

- 219 -

COLLECTING COVERS

A cover, when referred to in the language of the stamp collecting fraternity, is technically an envelope upon which is an address and a stamp or a postal marking to indicate postage paid or due, and the cancellation required which indicates the date and place of mailing and, oftentimes, a back stamp to show date of arrival in the delivery area. "On Cover" is also used as a term to indicate that a specific stamp is on a cover; it could be on a postcard or an envelope but it would be on an original sending.

For many years cover collecting had been somewhat neglected due in part to the many sizes of envelopes which have been used over the years. Stamp collectors today have well realized the philatelic and the historical importance in having covers of their choice in their stamp collections, as well as the high regard with which covers are considered by those who do philatelic research.

There are specific albums designed to house cover collections, they range in size from those to accommodate the normal size of envelope to those of the larger oversize envelope. It is not to be said that a cover collection is always the neatest collection to arrange because some envelopes are slit open at the top, some at the sides, and still others are just torn open. They may look ragged or tatty, but the stamps, the cancellations or other postal markings are still the key reasons for them to be retained in collections.

Building a collection of covers requires patience and a good feeling for the hunt and search. One just does not go into a store and buy whatever covers he wishes. A collector may search through the cover stocks of a dozen different dealers and not find one cover which will interest him; on the other hand, he might find one dealer who could supply him with a dozen or more!

To form a really nice collection of covers, and to become properly oriented in this phase of collecting, a collector should subscribe to "COVERS MAGAZINE," published by Western Stamp Collector in Albany, Oregon.

The following illustrations show covers which have gone through war, occupation, strained border relations, fieldposts, etc., and are just a few samples of the thousands of covers available to stamp collectors who wish to "educate" their stamp collections.

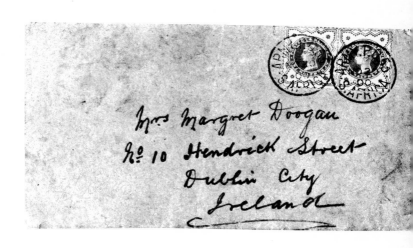

Here is a good example of British stamps being used abroad. This cover was mailed from the British Army Post Office No. 53 in South Africa on November 20, 1900, to Ireland.

This cover was mailed in Arequipa, Peru, during the War of the Pacific between Chile and Peru, 1879-82. The stamp is a provisional issue of 10 centavos, originally bisected to be used as 5 centavos.

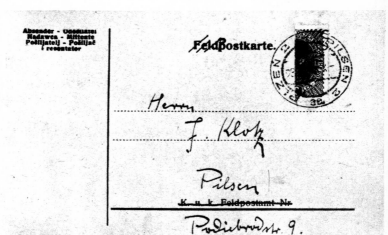

A former Austrian military fieldpost card; the sender marked out the "Feld" (Field) as well as the "K. u K. Feldpostamt Nr." (King and Kingdom Fieldpost station Number), and mailed it in December 1918 with Christmas greetings. Austrian stamp bisected with "FRANCO" overprint.

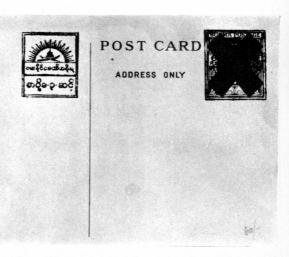

An unused postcard from Burma. The original imprinted stamp showed the crowned head of King George VI which was defaced with a blue X and an overprint of the Burma Peacock during the Japanese occupation of Burma, World War II.

This cover was mailed from the Portuguese colony of Lourenco Marques to Capetown, South Africa, during the Boer War. It was opened by the British military censor and resealed with the martial law label.

Here is a cover from the Russo-Japanese War, postmarked 26-5-04 Liaoyang Field Post Office "a" with registration label. It was received in Moscow on 15-6-04.

During World War I many German military and government personnel in the Orient were taken into custody by the Japanese. This cover is from the Matsuyama prison camp in Japan, mailed in 1917 to Berlin, Germany, and was censored.

Cancellation from a German submarine, WWI.

Capt Cooper
1st Sikhs
Tartar City
Peking

This cover is a real philatelic classic. The allied nations in China asked the British military forces there to administrate the railway between Shanhaikwan and Peking immediately after the Boxer riots of 1901. In order to expedite soldiers' mail, the British attached a mail van to this train to handle the soldiers' mail. The charge was 5 cents for each letter posted at Shanhaikwan, Tonshan, Tongku, Tientsin and Peking. The ½¢ brown stamp of China has been surcharged "B.R.A. (for British Railway Authority) 5 five cents" for the extra charge. The purple cancellation reads "Railway Post Office, Tientsin," the India stamp overprinted C.E.F. (Chinese Expeditionary Forces) is cancelled April 26, 1901. The B.R.A. overprinted and surcharged stamp was in use for only one month, April 20 to May 20, after which the mail service was free.

This postcard from the former German colony of Caroline Islands in the Pacific Ocean has a bisected 10 pf stamp in order to pay the 5 pf postal rate. A typhoon destroyed the stock of 5 pf stamps and so the 10 pf stamps were cut in half.

This cover was mailed from the Turkish Empire as backstamped departure from Istanbul on November 26, 1915, and was received in Berlin on December 7, 1915.

Cancellation from Berlin Airlift.

This cover is from the Russian Refugees' Post, under General Baron Peter Wrangel. Mailed from Tuzla (Turkey) to Galipoli (Turkey) on April 8, 1921. It arrived in Galipoli on April 15, 1921. The stamp is a 3 kopec imperial arms design of Russia, with trident overprint for the Ukraine, and surcharged 10,000 rubles for the use of the Wrangel Army.

This postcard was mailed Oct. 24, 1905, during the Russo-Japanese War, by the Secretary of the Army Staff of French Occupation Corps in Tientsin, China. Arrived in Liege, Belgium, March 28, 1906.

This is a native handmade cover from Wuchang, China, 1903. An additional cancellation reads Hankow. Backstamped at Peking.

POSTAL STATIONERY

When referring to postal stationery we are not thinking of postage stamps on cover or postcards, but rather of specially printed letter sheets, postcards, envelopes, wrappers, aerograms, etc., which have their individual stamp design and postal value printed on a specific type of stationery required for the specified use of the denomination.

It will be noticed immediately that many designs of the stamp imprint on different types of postal sationery are the same as those used for the postage stamps printed in sheets. This was done for economic reasons as well as to maintain the image of national designs, or a ruling family, international recognition of the country of origin, etc.

For those collectors who would enjoy collecting postal stationery along with their stamp collections, it is recommended that they become a member of the Postal History Society of the Americas by contacting Theodore Van Dam, Secretary, at 1122 East 180th Street, Bronx, New York 10460. The official magazine of this society is most informative and will be of considerable interest to all collectors.

Postal stationery collecting has been somewhat dormant in the wide world of stamp collecting ever since stationery was omitted from the Scott Standard Postage Stamp Catalogue. The last edition of Scott's Catalogue to carry worldwide postal stationery was in 1904 and since then there have been only those catalogues printed in Germany or France after WWI, but these are difficult to acquire because of such limited printings. There is now however, a new Catalogue of the Postal Stationery of the World by Higgins & Gage of Pasadena, California. This catalogue is being published in loose-leaf format, alphabetically arranged by countries, and they are using the fine old Ascher catalogue as a basic foundation for this new edition. The editors are bringing to the American public a much needed and long awaited priced and illustrated catalogue of worldwide postal stationery.

The following illustrations depict a few designs of postcards, envelopes, lettercards, wrappers, etc., which point up the great historical value of these related philatelic items:

ZUID-AFRIK. REPUBLIEK
RÉPUBLIQUE SUD-AFRICAINE
Algemeene Post-Vereeniging — (Union Postale Universelle)

BRIEFKAART
(Carte postale)

Poſtkarte

Poſtkarte mit Antwortkarte
Carte postale avec réponse payée

UNION POSTALE UNIVERSELLE
BILHETE POSTAL

Correspondencia   Endereço

UNION POSTALE UNIVERSELLE

ST. HELENA .

POST CARD

HE ADDRESS ONLY TO BE WRITTEN ON THIS SIDE.

BREVKORT.

INLAND

POST CARD

TRINIDAD

THE ADDRESS ONLY TO BE WRITTEN ON THIS SIDE.

1878

878

Deze omslagen kunnen alleen gebruikt worden voor Nieuwsbladen of voor zoodanige artikelen, die tegen boekpost-tarief verzonden kunnen worden, en mogen geen brief of mededeeling, in den vorm van een brief, inhouden. — Indien in strijd met bovenstaande gehandeld wordt, zal het pakket als brief worden aangemerkt, en dienovereenkomstig worden belast. —

Aan

Postkarte
Weltpostverein
Carte postale
Union postale universelle

BRITISH GUIANA REGISTERED LETTER.

THIS LETTER MUST BE GIVEN TO AN OFFICER OF THE POST OFFICE
TO BE REGISTERED, AND A RECEIPT BE OBTAINED FOR IT.

THE STAMP
TO PAY THE
POSTAGE
MUST BE
PLACED HERE.

Brev-Kort.

(Paa denne Side skrives kun Adressen.)

Til

St. Domingo

UNION POSTAL UNIVERSAL

TARJETA POSTAL

REPUBLICA DOMINICANA

DIOS PATRIA LIBERTAD

2 DOS CENTAVOS 2

REPUBLIQUE DOMINICAINE

ESCRIBASE DE ESTE LADO LA DIRECCION Y LA COMUNICACION DEL OTRO.

UNION POSTALE UNIVERSELLE

THE HALNATTAN BANK NOTE CO. NEW YORK.

TONGA
LETTER CARD

LETTER CARD

POST CARD

THE ADDRESS ONLY TO BE WRITTEN ON THIS SIDE.

The price is
Three cents
including the Card.

2½ cents

TO OPEN CUT HERE

AEROGRAM

LUFTPOST
PAR AVION

TO OPEN CUT HERE

5

Deutſche Reichspoſt

Poſtkarte

An

UNION POSTALE UNIVERSELLE

BRITISH NEW GUINEA

OST CARD CARTE POSTALE

THE ADDRESS ONLY TO BE WRITTEN ON THIS SIDE.

UNION POSTALE UNIVERSELLE

BRITISH HONDURAS (HONDURAS BRITANNIQUE)

POST CARD.

THE ADDRESS ONLY TO BE WRITTEN ON THIS SIDE.

~~UNION POSTALE UNIVERSELLE~~

POST CARD ~~GREAT BRITAIN & IRELAND~~

BRITISH PROTECTORATE

~~(GRANDE BRETAGNE ET IRLANDE)~~

OIL RIVERS

THE ADDRESS ONLY TO BE WRITTEN ON THIS SIDE.

1278608

TARJETA POSTAL

REPLY POST CARD.

THE ADDRESS ONLY TO BE WRITTEN ON THIS SIDE.

පිට ලියන නම පමණක් මේ පැත්තේ ලියනු.

மேல்விலாசத்தைமாத்திரம் இந்தப்பக்கத்தி லெழுதவும்.

CEYLON
2c.
POSTAGE

To

POST ✪ CARD

GIBRALTAR

THE ADDRESS ONLY TO BE WRITTEN ON THIS SIDE.

HALFPENNY

MASHONALAND

INLAND POST CARD
THE ADDRESS ONLY TO BE WRITTEN ON THIS SIDE.

A. Ran. Esq.

Buluwayo.

ᴊᴏ 015866 ✳

TARJETA POSTAL
ZONA DE PROTECTORADO ESPAÑOL EN MARRUECOS

A _____

UNION POSTALE UNIVERSELLE
SARAWAK
POST CARD
THE ADDRESS ONLY TO BE WRITTEN ON THIS SIDE.

POST CARD

KENYA AND UGANDA
THE ADDRESS ONLY TO BE WRITTEN ON THIS SIDE

This Wrapper may only be used for Newspapers or for
such documents as are allowed to be sent at the Book-rate
of postage, and must not enclose any letter or communication
of the nature of a letter (whether separate or otherwise).
If this rule be infringed, the packet will be charged as a letter.

TOPICAL STAMP COLLECTING

Most stamp collectors have a favorite topic or theme which they enjoy keeping in a special collection. The topical collector often has several favorite subjects or topics and the list of topics can go on into the hundreds. The field is so large that one might wonder where to begin. There is no set point of beginning because a topic that strikes the fancy of one collector may not interest another at all. The best way to really get started in Topical Collecting is to join the American Topical Society which already has over 8,000 members who collect over 700 different topics. A letter to the Executive Secretary, Jerome Husak at 3306 North 50th Street, Milwaukee, Wisconsin 53216, will bring all the necessary information and an application form to become a member for a modest fee. Through the American Topical Society the collector may obtain numerous handbooks and special guide books of many different topics as well as the monthly magazine "TOPICAL TIMES." Every collector would find this to be the start of a truly great philatelic adventure and I heartily recommend this organization to one and all.

A little review of just one topic is in order and so we go down to the sea where sailed the ships of many lands through centuries past. There are many hundreds of stamps which have a ship or a boat as the central design and the collector will be able to classify the ships into such categories as sailing ships, freighters, ocean liners, naval vessels, ice-breakers, schooners, yachts, etc.

Illustrated here are some of the stamps from various countries which lend credence to the lure of the sea:

GERMAN KINDERPOST (Children's Post)

During the late 19th century when the German Empire was rapidly expanding abroad, the German businessmen were developing many new products at home. Their ability to lead the world in the manufacture of toys and children's games led them to conceive what is known as "KINDERPOST." This was originally nothing more than a game of post office for children which consisted of a selection of miniature envelopes, note paper, "stamps" and a small pillar (or post) box.

The philatelic interest in Kinderpost is in the miniature "stamps" which were part of the game and which were exact miniatures of the real stamps in use by the government. The poignant interest in the illustrations which follow is that the Kinderpost "stamp" was "used" on a letter from a child to her father in the German Army, mailed on May 23, 1916, 10-11 A.M.

PHILATELIC LITERATURE

Another exciting and romantic phase of stamp collecting is the acquisition of a good philatelic background by reading books and reference works. This cannot be accomplished in any short period of time because it means building a library of books, references and magazines on stamps and stamp collecting as well as keeping a reference of stamp club publications so that all of this printed material is available for ready reference.

During the past 80 years there have been thousands of these reference books, handbooks, guidebooks, magazines and club publications, etc., which have been written by people who loved their hobby of stamp collecting and who presented hitherto unknown facts and points of information. These books and articles have contributed immensely to the pleasure and the satisfaction of relaxation that is so highly regarded today in the wide world of stamp collecting.

The easiest way to build a nicely rounded library suited to the desire of the individual collector is to join the Philatelic Literature Association. The editor is Daniel W. Vooys, at Post Office Box 187, Canajoharie, New York 13317. This organization publishes a quarterly magazine which is very well edited and prepared with reviews of new books, catalogues, etc., as well as a section devoted to a listing of books for sale and a listing of books wanted by members. There are also advertisements from auctioneers who handle philatelic literature auction sales periodically as well as make a specialty of selling philatelic reference works.

A stamp collector has no better friends than the books in his philatelic library, and he can turn to these books at any time of day or night to check or review his thoughts or just to chat with the author from long ago. Very few of the philatelic reference books are dull or dry or written above the average person. On the contrary they are mostly written in the vein of telling a story or of explaining an interesting reason why certain events took place, or how the stamps came to be issued, etc. It is always good to remember that we learn from what someone else learned and thought enough of to put into print.

A most important part of any collector's library is always his choice of a standard postage stamp catalogue. There are many standard catalogues because, for example, in France the collector uses Catalogue Yvert-Tellier, Catalogue Thiaude, Berck, etc.; in Spain they use Galvez Catalogue; in Germany they use Michel Katalog, Senf and Zumstein. In Switzerland the Zumstein is standard. In England and throughout the British Empire the perennial favorite—The Stanley Gibbons Catalogues are the standard works. And so it goes; almost every area has a particular type of standard catalogue, but all the while the Stanley Gibbons Catalogues are more often referred to. The Stanley Gibbons Catalogues are recognized the world over for reliability, completeness, knowledgeable editing and classification, having been first published in 1865 and continued to grow and expand to the point that today they are really world renowned.

In the U.S.A. for more than 90 years the Scott Standard Postage Stamp Catalogues have reigned most successfully, even though there

Philatelic Literature,

is not the listing or pricing of the many varieties and local and semi-official stamps as one finds in the catalogues printed in other countries. Also by Scott Publications is the United States Stamp Catalogue, Specialized. This most comprehensive book is invaluable to the collector of United States postage stamps, revenues, postal stationery, Confederate States, and United States possessions including Hawaii, Puerto Rico, Philippine Commonwealth, Canal Zone, etc. The Minkus New World Wide Stamp Catalogs made their appearance more than 10 years ago. The historical information and the explanations of the stamp designs are of particular interest to the topical collector as well as the specialist. There are probably more minor varieties and types of local and semi-official stamps listed and priced than in any other postage stamp catalogue printed in the English language. The Minkus New American Stamp Catalog is also packed with information regarding the designs, the commemorative issues, etc., of the U.S.A. in sufficient detail as to make it a must for all philatelic libraries.

It is very important for the collector to use catalogue numbers in keeping his checklist, or record of costs, or inventory, or when ordering stamps from dealers. All uses of catalogue numbers must be designated to a specific catalogue, such as Gibbons, or Scott, or Minkus. This eliminates any chance of error or confusion when the dealer starts to fill the order or send out a selection of specific stamps. This also applies to those collectors who write up their collections for display at stamp conventions or at stamp clubs.

STAMP CLUBS

Do not be mislead into thinking that you would never get anything out of being a member of a stamp club!

In the wide world of stamps today all of us can find something to learn every day. A good stamp club tries to maintain a philatelic library as well as a roster of good and interesting collector-speakers who can either regale the membership or hold them spellbound with their philatelic adventures, experiences and discoveries. There are very many stamp clubs throughout the U.S.A. and it would just not be possible to list them all. But to touch on one or two areas would not be amiss. In Seattle, Washington, a collector would meet many specialists in the stamps of Scandinavian countries, in Chicago a collector would meet many specialists in the stamps of Poland, Greece and Germany and German States. Whenever these specialists are the feature of a program for a stamp club meeting there is usually an overflow of members who want to hear what is being presented. This again is how we all learn.

There are many large stamp clubs that have branches in other cities and states, and the parent club issues a regular magazine pertaining to the events of the particular club or specialty.

The American Philatelic Society is the great national organization, and here too the collector member receives a monthly journal which is packed with vital information for collectors of all ages. The editor is: James M. Chemi, at 5932 North 14th Place, Phoenix, Arizona 85014.

BIBLIOGRAPHY

CATALOGUES, BOOKS,
MAGAZINES, ETC.:
Australian Stamp Monthly
French Philatelic Facts
Stanley Gibbons of London Stamp
   Monthly, from 1890
Stanley Gibbons of London
   Standard Catalogues
Mekeel's Magazine, from 1897
Michel Catalogue
Minkus New Worldwide Catalogues
Philatelic Exporter
Scott Standard Postage
   Stamp Catalogues
Stamps Magazine
Western Stamp Collector
Yvert Tellier Catalogue
Zumstein Catalogue

AUCTION CATALOGUES:
Ebel
Gibbons
Harmer

Harmer Rooke
Lowe
Mohrmann
Rigby
Vlastos
etc.

PUBLICATIONS OF SOCIETIES
AND GROUPS
American Philatelic Journal
Anglo-Boer War Club
The China Society
International Society of Japanese
   Philately Bulletin
The London Philatelist
Netherlands and Colonies Society
Orange Free State Study Circle
Philately from Australia
The Postal Bell
Postal Stationary Society
Spanish Civil War Club
Topical Times
Transvaal Study Circle

INDEX

For additional detailed information see the Philatelic Glossary Section starting on page 172.

—250—

—253—